Bant

*'A serious and good philosophical work
could be written consisting entirely of jokes.'*

– LUDWIG WITTGENSTEIN

Bantaism

THE PHILOSOPHY OF SARDAR JOKES

Bhai Niranjan Singh 'Amrikawale'

RUPA

First published in 2011 by
Rupa Publications India Pvt. Ltd.
7/16, Ansari Road, Daryaganj
New Delhi 110002

Sales centres:

Allahabad Bengaluru Chennai
Hyderabad Jaipur Kathmandu
Kolkata Mumbai

ISBN: 978-81-291-1889-9

10 9 8 7 6 5 4 3 2

Niranjan Ramakrishnan asserts the moral right to be identified
as the author of this work.

Printed in India by
Rekha Printers Pvt Ltd.
A-102/1, Okhla Industrial Area, Phase-II
New Delhi 110 020

To the memory of *D Subbarao*
Physicist, Philosopher, Connoisseur, Friend

A Note on the Notables

A few eminent public figures appear in these jokes. The stories in this book, including those involving them, are apocryphal, in no way to be confused with real-life personas.

Author's Note

I couldn't have been more than seven or eight when I heard my first sardar[1] joke. It opened for me, as someone said of PG Wodehouse's novels, 'a world to live and delight in'. I have treasured ever since each gem that has come my way.

But it was only in college several years later that I first ran across Banta Singh. He figured in some jokes told by a Punjabi classmate, an outstanding raconteur. Incidentally, Banta's associate those days was Bachittar Singh not Santa, just as his wife bore the stately name of Kulwant Kaur instead of the Preeto or Jeeto she has since become. In time this new character, like Mulla Nasruddin or Father Brown, would come to acquire a universal persona all his own.

The invention of Banta Singh seems to have achieved two purposes. For the joke-teller, the very name is a godsend. It trips off the tongue. It is delightfully rustic, rotund, funny, broadly benign with a whiff of low craft – a concoction guaranteed to provoke a laugh just by its mention. Its other task, perhaps not originally envisaged, is as a fig-leaf in our increasingly touchy

---

[1]Sardar is a term used for 'leader' or 'head' or 'chief' in many parts of Asia, including Afghanistan, Pakistan and India. In India it is mainly used for adult male members in Sikh families.

times – to provide a pretense that this is not really about sardars; it is just about one lone guy called Banta Singh. I've always thought this was a pathetic cop-out, even disingenuous. Banta Singh without the 'sardar' identity is like Hamlet without the Prince of Denmark. Banta is to Sardardom what Homer Simpson is to America, a caricature entirely imperfect but wholly irresistible; Homer is certainly not America, but you cannot conceive of his being from anywhere else.

Meanwhile that traditional staple, *ik vaari ik* sardar *si* ... (once there was a sardar ...) – the Classic Coke of the sardar joke – continues to march along, as everyone knows it will: some jokes are just naturally *ik vaari ik* sardar *si's*. And Banta Singh too is here to stay; with a name like his it could not be otherwise. Both have their own place, and that's all there is to it. How does one decide when to use which? For a hint of how to resolve such conundrums we have only to look to the master himself:

'*Oye Banteya*, how do you tell whether a chick is a *murga* (rooster) or *murgi* (hen)?' someone once asked Banta Singh.

'*Koi vaddi gal nahin* (it's no big deal). I feed it some rice and then observe carefully,' replied Banta, '*je khaooga ta murga e, je khaoogi ta murgi e* (if *he* eats it, it's a rooster, if *she* eats it, it's a hen).'

From whom to feature in a sardar joke we move to a more fraught question: whether to tell a sardar joke. With all due respect to the Political Correctness Police, I think it is an insult to the average citizen to say he needs to be shielded from certain kinds of jokes on the chance that he may believe something he hears as the gospel truth (an especially lame plea in an era when even the gospel has trouble passing as the gospel truth). The simplest of folk have sophistication enough to separate the real nature of individuals/communities from the apocrypha about them. For me this was brought home – not literally, for all my jokes came from friends and classmates and other adults outside – early. I noticed even as a youngster that, while all kinds of people regaled one another with sardar jokes, Sikhs were in general well regarded. They were seldom addressed other than as 'sardarji', and treated with a respect sometimes bordering on deference and awe, stemming perhaps in part from some feeling of guilt.

Of their reputation for physical bravery, courage and sacrifice, no Indian needs to be told; a cursory acquaintance with history would do. But growing up in New Delhi with its large Sikh population I came to learn that they also tended to be among India's most hard-working, open, and large-hearted citizens, albeit quick to anger.

The urban Sikh was not unoften the most urbane of Indians. It was even reputed that many sardar jokes were made up by sardars themselves. Impossible to verify, of course, but if true there can be no greater tribute to the sardar intelligence. Or self-confidence. I do know that the use of expressions like, '*Oye toon aadmi hai ki* sardar (are you human or sardar)', or '*sardaraan waali gal* (sardar logic)' was common in gently debunking any perceived infirmities of reason. That such things could be said as freely to a Sikh, even inviting a smiling repartee on occasion, '*Oye jaddon hain hi* sardar *ta sardaraan waali gal kivain nahin karaange* (when one is a sardar, after all, how would one not talk sardarspeak)?' said volumes about the self-esteem and sense of humor of the Sikh. Indians are usually happiest making fun of everyone else while wearing the thinnest of skins themselves. Sikhs seemed to be a wonderful exception to this norm.

Into this happy world some unknown public school lads of the 1960s introduced another term: Surd. My guess is that it came out of SL Loney's classic text on mathematics. The word originally meant irrational number. Given the nature of the sardar joke, it is easy to imagine that this fact must have struck its purveyors as a serendipity exceeding their wildest dreams. Whatever its etymology, 'Surd' soon gained currency in city school and college campuses, at least the English-breathing ones. The chai shop near the IIT Delhi campus, for instance, was known as 'Surd Shop' because it was run by a sardar. No one gave it a second thought (no pun intended).

All this easy back and forth started to change in the early 1980s. The Indian government got involved in a dangerous game, playing with fire for nothing more than a transient political advantage. They tried to offset their mainstream political opponents in Punjab by encouraging the most obscurantist (and mostly humorless) fringes within the Sikh community. What followed was a decade-and-a-half of pure tragedy, human and political, an effort by enemies of India 'to alienate Sikhs from Hindus, and to alienate them from the Indian state' (quoting roughly from what an Indian journalist wrote at that time). This is not the place to get into the march of crime and folly by the Indian government, the murderous violence by the Sikh terrorists, the harassment of Sikhs during the 1982 Asiad, the army raid on the Golden Temple, Prime Minister Indira Gandhi's killing, the anti-Sikh pogrom that followed, and the abuses perpetrated by all sides on Punjab for the next decade.

From the viewpoint of sardar joke, this traumatic time saw a progressive thinning of the Sikh skin, a rise in intolerance, the surfacing of an uncharacteristic atavism and the appearance of one sure sign of a diminished self-esteem – a perpetual ear cocked for slights real and imagined. For good measure many of these developments received encouragement from some Sikhs abroad. It is paradoxical that the progressiveness of a community in India appears these days to be in inverse proportion to how many of its numbers are settled in the West!

I received something by way of an explanation many years ago from a niece of Sardar Swaran Singh, former defense and external affairs minister of India. I ran into her not in India but in Vancouver, BC, where she lived. Her father (Swaran Singh's elder brother) had settled there in 1903! She said that emigrants like her tended to 'hold on' to an India that may no longer exist.

All said and done, I feel that the Sikh in India is far less insecure than his cohorts in the UK, USA or Canada. Yet, the Indian Sikh was the primary victim of many crimes leading to death, dismemberment or disruption in Punjab, instigated and carried out at the behest of some among these same immigrant communities in the name of 'honor' or 'dignity'. There is little more heinous than fostering mayhem from a safe distance, worse, for nothing more than perceived injury to pride. Often these are also the same folk who express elaborate hurt at some imagined slight in the lands of their domicile. Long years of exposure to the putative openness and tolerance of the West appears to have had little impact. A few years ago, a play scheduled to open in the UK had to be canceled and the playwright and actors reportedly went into hiding, because of death threats from some

Sikh groups who found the drama's theme objectionable. The British government, whose duty one presumes is to protect the lives, liberties and freedom of expression of its citizens, appeared to be helpless, or simply not to care.

The way I see it, every part of the world has its own favorite ethnic/professional/sectional joke. In Delhi, where I grew up, it was the sardar joke. Later, as I was exposed to humor from other regions of the globe, it was clear that jokes traveled, with the character modified to suit the locale. Figuratively then, Mulla Nasruddin might discard the thobe and get into a pair of slacks to figure in the Polish joke, then don a turban and beard for his forthcoming trip to Delhi or Amritsar. The genius of the joke lay as much in the cleverness of adaptation as in its essence.

Why this book? I have spent the major portion of my career in the software world. In the course of my work I was surprised to find that a number of illustrative examples pertaining to conceptual, design and business issues could be drawn directly from sardar jokes. Later I discovered the same thing with some of my writings on politics and current affairs (as the saying goes, to a man with a hammer everything begins to look like a nail – maybe I'd heard too many sardar jokes).

Still, one is frequently dumbstruck at finding some patently implausible *chutkula*[2] being enacted almost verbatim, not by Banta and Bachittar but by supposedly wise world-statesmen. It slowly dawned on me that the sardar joke was a lot bigger than the garden-variety gag. Instead, it was showing itself to be deep, philosophical, profound, and universal!

---

[2]Joke

If the American baseball star Yogi Berra can be called a philosopher and have his sayings celebrated as Yogi-isms, is there any reason why our own Banta Singh's glories cannot spawn their unique brand of wisdom? To reach for that most elemental of tenets from the Punjabi weltanschauung, *'Assi kede maade haan* (why are *we* any less)?' Thus Bantaism.

Kipling wrote, 'What do they know of England who only England know.' So it is with those who think the sardar joke is about the sardar. In my own case I've found myself identifying with practically every variety of folly in every sardar joke. I seem to have replicated many if not most of them. Often the jokes are but send-ups of a mind fixed in its ways and resistant to any but its own accustomed modes of operation. Nor can I boast of being so far outside the mainstream as to claim any exclusive ownership of such debacles. I feel certain that we have all had our share of set ways, blinkered reasoning and associated lunacies. Through the rustic foibles of Banta and his friends, we are gently reminded that the joke really is on us and all our pretensions. To paraphrase the headline in a French newspaper the morning after 9/11: WE ARE ALL SARDARS NOW.[3] Or if you prefer, *'Hun assaan saare Bante haan'* (we are all Banta Singhs now).'

Another thing to keep in mind. Several jokes that did not appear to me very deep at the outset took on a definite philosophical hue over time – sometimes with a startling suddenness. That is, I had to grow mature enough to 'get it'. This process may itself be best illustrated by – *what else?* – a sardar joke heard long ago, told by a sardarni[4] at a social gathering,

---

[3]'We Are All Americans Now', *Le Monde*, 12 Sep 2001.
[4]Sikh lady.

to the laughter of her heart-patient father, her mother, and her husband, all Sikhs:

> When the Alfred Hitchcock thriller *Psycho* came to town, everyone was eager to see it, including the sardarji. His family was totally opposed to the idea, though, because he had a serious heart condition and had been advised against undue excitement or shock. But he was insistent, and in the end they were forced to take him along when they went to see the film.
>
> To everyone's surprise, he did just fine after seeing *Psycho*. Then one fine day, three months later, he died suddenly of a heart attack.
>
> Word on the street was that the sardar had died as soon as he understood the movie (*jiddon* picture *samajh aaya taan hune mar gaya*).

My aim with this book is threefold: To capture the best sardar jokes, to examine their deeper meaning, and to make their narration easy.

How should you read a book like this? My only advice is, go slow. Imagine the characters, visualize the situation, and roll the words over. And remember, no more than one or two jokes a day. Give it time. Let it settle. Like enjoying fine wine, to 'vail thee full ban-fit,'[5] the sardar joke too must be savored on many levels. The true connoisseur will let a picture settle in his imagination, let the words sprinkle over it, then allow the whole scenario to run through his head a few times, until without his knowing a smile spreads slowly across his face. There is no feeling equal to it.

---

[5]Tr: Avail of the full benefit.

Should you decide to tell sardar jokes, it is best to get some practice first. To get you started, the jokes in this book are written as they might be read out to an audience.

You'll get a little more out of the book and a lot more out of your renditions if you can read the Punjabi (you don't have to know the language) out loud. I've tried to supply the words and the translation, but reading out the English in a suitable cadence is often perfectly adequate.

Translating the Punjabi *gaali*[6] is a different matter, however, for it is its own wonderland. Here you will have to manage without my help. Wherever you see something like ^&%$^, use your imagination – freely, but knowing you may yet fall short.

A final note: The book contains some of my favorite sardar jokes, but not one of these is my own. I have merely gathered them, lovingly over the years, from friends and colleagues, and in more recent times from email forwards. My only claim to originality lies in the titles, the retelling, and observations which, where I have any, are provided immediately following the joke. As you read I'm sure you will have your own epiphanies (well, epi-funnies, at any rate).

Enjoy (*oye just enjway*)!

Niranjan Ramakrishnan
New Delhi
May 2010

---

[6]Punjabi, the language spoken by most Sikhs, is famous for its rich and colorful swear words and oaths, known as *gaalis*. Technically, *gaali* is a Hindi word, the Punjabi word for it is *gaal*. Cultural socio-linguists may make what they will out of the fact that it differs by a single letter from the word *gal* (pronounced as in seagull), which is the Punjabi for 'talk' or 'matter'.

The Meaning of Everysingh

To my mind the deepest of all sardar jokes is the one about the train journey.

Which one, you will ask. As any connoisseur of sardar jokes knows, the Indian Railways form the supporting cast for so many. While this is undeniable (e.g., see pages 30, 44, 88), for sheer insight this one is Singh, er ... King.

It all begins with the Bombay Mail as it is pulling out of the New Delhi railway station. Passengers are still putting away their luggage. Once this is done they settle down and survey their fellow *yatris*[1] on the overnight trip to Bombay. They note that their little klatch of eight (upper, middle and lower on both sides, plus an upper and lower along the passage) consists of not just one but two sardars, one wearing a red turban and the other a green.

Our correspondent permits himself a smile as he contemplates the sight of the two gentlemen leaning out of the train doorway from time to time for a spot of breeze, and the engine driver mistaking the colors to halt or start the train at random. And what would happen if both red and green leaned out at once? Would the driver stop, or go?

---

[1]Hindi for traveler or passenger.

But that's not the story.

After the first snacks have been consumed and the chai-wala has made his round, some tentative get-acquainted conversations begin.

The green sardar turns to the red one and asks, 'Are you going up to Bombay?'

Red: 'Yes, that's where I'm going.'

Green: 'Dadar or Bombay Central?'

Red: 'Dadar.'

Green: 'Aha, same here.'

Red: 'You are visiting Bombay or you live there?'

Green: 'Visiting, visiting. I live here in K'rol Bagh.[2] I'm going to Bombay for my nephew's marriage.'

Red: 'Arre, I live in K'rol Bagh, and I'm going for a marriage too. Where in K'rol Bagh are you, incidentally?'

Green: '8A Block.'

Red: 'Amazing! Same block as me.'

The two shake hands as a neighborly gesture.

Green: '*Gazab di gal hai* (remarkable). Such a coincidence! Here we are, two people in a train compartment, from the same block in Karol Bagh, both going to Bombay, and that too for a wedding!'

By now the other passengers are mildly curious. One of them ventures, 'What about you, sardarji, where is the wedding in Bombay?'

Green: 'Day after tomorrow, in Andheri.'[3]

Red: '*Lo ji ae vi k'maal hai* (this is a wonder too), the one I'm going to is also in Andheri, and day after tomorrow!'

Green: 'And when are you returning to Delhi?'

---

[2] A neighborhood in New Delhi.
[3] A neighborhood in Mumbai.

Red: 'I have a ticket on the same train the day after the wedding.'

Green: What a wonder, me too!

Red: Maybe we can take a taxi together, where are you staying in Andheri?

Green: 'Mehrban Towers. It's just off the main road. You can't miss it.'

Red: 'I won't miss it. That's exactly where I'm staying too. Which floor?'

Green: 'Sixth, I think.'

Red: 'This is really too much. I think I'm on the same floor too.'

On and on this sequence of coincidences grows, till it is discovered that the two work in the same business, live in the same building in Delhi, buy milk from the same booth down the street ...

By now the entire compartment is riveted by this almost astronomical improbability happening before their eyes.

One passenger finally blurts out, 'This is real *maya*. What a *karishma* (wonder), you live in the same locality, you are going together, coming back together, both to attend a wedding, staying in the same building, and returning by the same train. I've got to tell my friends about this. And yet you are meeting for the first time!'

The sardars pipe up, smiling, 'Actually we are father and son. We live in the same house and are going to attend the same wedding, and also coming back together by the same compartment on the same train.'

'We just like to make conversation like this to pass time on long train journeys,' he concluded.

Commentary

A little reflection will show that what the two sardars are doing is nothing more than a microcosm of the world. All the business and bustle around our existence is but a contrivance. We too, like the father and son above, make up our own joys and sorrows, our own 'conversations', to pass time during our sojourn on earth. We attribute meaning to things, ascribe values, apportion blame, all based on a made-up edifice of ethics and morals – made up entirely by us, that is.

When challenged we fall back upon language, as though it too is not our own creation. 'When I use a word, it means just what I choose it to mean, neither more or less.' These are Humpty Dumpty's words from *Through the Looking Glass*, and they apply to everything we speak.

Artificial Intelligence (AI) pioneer and Massachusetts Institute of Technology (MIT) professor Marvin Minsky[4] wrote a book many years ago called, *The Society of Mind*. Another AI book talks of *The Meaning of Meaning*. The two sardars had arrived at similar conclusions independently.

The point is – all meaning is of our own construction. Consider this: Six-year-old Bobby is invited to his friend's birthday party next door. A formal invitation card arrives by the mail, along with an enclosed RSVP card and post-paid envelope. Bobby's parents have him write an equally formal acceptance note in return. On the appointed hour, little Bobby reaches his friend's party, present in tow, which he formally hands over. At the end of the party, the birthday kid's mom hands out goody bags to all the young guests. On reaching

---

[4]Minsky is best known for his Theory of Frames, a widely-used idea in constructing natural language simulations in Artificial Intelligence.

home, Bobby calls to thank his friend for the wonderful surprise in the goody bag ... A day later, a letter arrives, thanking Bobby for his lovely present. Both the families spend considerable amounts of time in this agonizing effort. The organizers of course have been at it for days together.

Is conducting a 'get-acquainted' conversation on a train that much more contrived? At least, without all the tinsel, torn packaging, thrown-away food and piled-up garbage a birthday party creates, the two sardars were enjoying themselves (and entertaining their fellow passengers at the same time) with scarcely a dent to the environment!

The Chai's is Yours

Banta Singh was sitting alone, enjoying a cup of tea at a restaurant. He couldn't help overhear the conversation at the next table, where a young man and woman, clearly in courtship, were seated.

The guy asked his lady friend, 'How many cups of tea can a person drink on an empty stomach?'

She thought for a while, stirring some sugar into her tea demurely, before replying, 'I guess three would be my answer.'

Her friend smiled and said slowly, 'You are wrong.'

'You asked me, and I told you,' said the girl, a little irritated. 'So what *is* the correct answer?'

'Don't get excited,' said the guy. 'Think about it. The correct answer is ... ONE,' he said. 'Once you have the first cup your stomach is no longer empty!' She laughed, and Banta Singh pondered over their conversation as they left the shop, hand in hand.

Such a nice joke. Something the wife would really enjoy, he said to himself.

That evening after supper he placed the matter squarely before her. 'Well, Jeeto, how many cups of tea can you have on an empty stomach?'

'I don't like tea,' she replied. 'After five years of marriage don't you even know that about me? Shows how much you care.'

The conversation was not going as planned.

He parried as best he could, telling her it was only a joke he had heard. 'Arre re re. What I mean is, if you did like tea, how many cups could you drink on an empty stomach?'

'*S'waal paida nahin honda jaddon* (the question doesn't arise when) I don't like it only.'

It took quite some persuasion, but finally he managed to cajole an answer out of her.

'Two,' she said.

Banta Singh could barely contain his exasperation. 'You stupid woman,' he hissed under his breath. Aloud he merely said, 'Tsk tsk tsk. Too bad. If only you had said "three" I would have told you such a nice joke ...'

Commentary

One moral is quite universal: We take things literally all the time, certainly more often than we realize. Devotion to trappings while missing the essence is at the root of innumerable problems, not alone those involving religion. Nor is this merely an artifact of language.

It is also what happens when we forget the original purpose of something, which happens often. This is true as much of human beings as of political parties. Over time, our sayings and responses become packaged, canned; our assumptions remain unexamined and we continue with them whether or not they hold water any more.

The mind is a lazy beast, and avoids soiling the synapses as much as it can. Assumption is its sustaining sponsor in this effort. The more we can assume, the less we need to think. A friend of mine has a saying worth keeping in mind: 'Assume makes an Ass of U and ME'.

Bearing in mind the result is often good enough, and much more convenient. But this works only as long as the assumption on which the result is based holds true. Over time we remember the formula but forget the assumption that makes it valid. Sometimes the process is benign: words like 'sandwich' or 'boycott' began life as proper nouns, but no one remembers their original sources any more. At other times, such as with the machinery whose design has been lost, the result can be disastrous. Forgetting assumptions is the cause of hundreds of industrial accidents each year.

Sher-e-Tronto

This is an ancient favorite; though ostensibly disparaging it carries several gems of insight.

In the early 1960s, when Indians were few and far between in Toronto, an early emigrant sardar had already been in Canada a couple of years working as an engineer. His luck did not hold, unfortunately, and his company had to lay him off. He lived as long as he could on his savings as he looked for another job, but times were tough and jobs hard to come by. Finally, he decided he could put it off no longer. Rather than return home defeated, he decided to jump off a bridge and end his life.

As he walked along the bridge to find a suitable spot, he noticed a man following him. At this point the man hailed him, and asked him about himself. Sardarji related his sad story. Asking him not to take any precipitate step, the man suggested they go someplace to sit down and talk over a cup of coffee and a sandwich (with him buying, naturally).

After they had warmed themselves by the fire and had a sip of coffee, the man began, 'You know, as soon as I saw you I had an idea. Now that you tell me you need a job, I feel we might actually be able to help each other.'

This was music to the sardar's ears.

'However,' continued the man, 'I don't want you to take this the wrong way because I don't mean to insult you. May I proceed?'

'Of course. Please carry on. I won't misunderstand.'

'Let me tell you a little story. You see, I'm the curator of our zoo here. Three years ago we got an Asian lion for our exhibit. It was the first lion the zoo had ever had, and it was a huge hit. Crowds lined up each evening and weekend, and it was the single biggest draw at the zoo.

'Now suddenly last week, the lion fell ill. The zoo doctor and I tried everything, but last night it died. This is still a secret, by the way. The public would be devastated if they come to know about the lion's death. I have a big problem on my hands. If people learn there is no lion, attendance at the zoo will drop, and we will have to close some exhibits laying off dozens of people. And we can't get another lion at short notice – there's a three-month wait. I'm at my wit's end. I've been roaming the streets all night racking my brains for a solution. Looking at you I suddenly had an idea. Again, please don't mistake me, and I say this in the best spirit.

'You, Mr Singh, bear a strong resemblance to that lion.'

The sardar was a little taken aback, but so earnest was the curator that he felt he should at least hear him out fully.

'OK? Now here's my idea,' the curator said, 'suppose I offered you the post of lion ...'

Before the sardar could protest he continued, 'Be assured, you will be well paid, plus receive free room and board, and you will make as much as you made in your last job, perhaps even more ...'

'And,' the curator went on, 'your exhibit only opens for three hours a day, so you just have three hours of work, when you will have to wear a lion's costume and prowl about the enclosure making suitably menacing gestures – hey, just like you're making now, that's beautiful!'

'And remember,' he proceeded before the sardar could open his mouth, 'on Mondays we are closed. So you will have plenty of time to look for another job while we find a real lion.'

Once his initial indignation had subsided, the sardarji was able to see the win-win nature of the proposition. He was a decisive man. 'OK,' he said, reaching to shake hands with the curator. 'I'll try it for three months.'

'That's the spirit,' the curator said, brightening for the first time during the entire conversation.

A man accustomed to doing whatever he undertook with gusto, the sardarji proved a true asset to the park. The new lion became an even bigger hit than the original one (not that anyone noticed the substitution, so convincing were the costume and the act). Soon the zoo was raking in even more admissions than ever before.

Two months passed. The curator had been as good as his word. It was just three hours a day, with a day off. Plenty of food, decent accommodation, and enough free time to search for a job, except, this job didn't seem so horrid any more after all...

Then one morning, upon entering his enclosure, he found that the adjoining cage, which had been empty, suddenly had inside it an enormous and fierce-looking Royal Bengal tiger whose roar seemed to rattle the roof. True, there were iron bars separating the two cages, but there was ever an element of fear in the sardarji's mind. It didn't help knowing that the animal next door could smell the difference between a man and a beast and was in no way fooled by the lion's costume. It growled and grimaced at the sardarji every time he looked at it.

Aeynihow (anyhow), a contract is a contract, he told himself as he plowed along, still a big draw albeit diminished somewhat by the new attraction next door.

But just a few days later, disaster struck.

Lost in worry one afternoon because he hadn't yet found a job, as he let himself into the enclosure, the sardarji found he had entered the tiger's cage by mistake, instead of his own. Only after the steel door had clanged shut behind him did he realize his error. Simultaneously, with a sinking feeling in his stomach he also knew it was too late to do anything about it.

The tiger, never a great fan of its neighbor, gave a series of blood-curdling growls from its corner, before slowly rising to its feet. Sardarji realized his only chance was to growl in response, lion-like, although he had not a shadow of a doubt the tiger knew very well he only was a puny human and not a lion. The beast was slowly advancing upon him. As it reached within five feet of him he knew in his heart that this was the end; it was only a matter of seconds before the huge claws tore him apart.

Sardarji decided to spend his last moments on earth taking the Lord's name. He closed his eyes and mumbled a prayer in Punjabi as he waited for the tiger to pounce.

His eyes were still shut when he heard a soft voice over the thud-thud-thud of his thumping heart, *'Assi Ambarsar de haan. Tussi kithoan* ... (I'm from Amritsar, and you are from ...)?'

Tailpiece: So great was the mutual relief that the two sardars embraced and shouted together in joy, *'Jo bole so nihal.'*

What followed was a reverberation of voices rising from every corner of the zoo, *'Sat Sri Akal!'*

Commentary

If you think this story offensive, you might like to consider what else call centers are about. Instead of Banta Singh or Bachittar Singh pretending to be tigers and lions, young men and women with names like Rahul and Sarita sit in Gurgaon and make believe that they are Mike and Sue parked in the Midwestern United States. In both cases they are fooling an unsuspecting audience, or so they like to think. Often it is when we are surest we are duping someone that the boot is most firmly on the other foot. A lot of business is like

11

that, with everyone going about with a mask on. And not just in business. In fact, as the old Raj Kapoor/Rajinder Kumar song has it, so is the entire world (the whole zoo?): *Do Jasoos/Kare Mehsoos/ Ke Duniya Badi Kharaab Hai/ Kaun Hai Sachcha/Kaun Hai Jhoota/Har Chehre Pe Nakaab hai.*[5]

Public Noo Ulloo

We are back to trains again.

The others in the compartment noticed that the sardarji reclining on the upper berth was doing something peculiar. Once every few minutes, he would take out a rail ticket (the old cardboard affair, not the new e-ticket) from his shirt pocket, hold it out in front of him between his thumb and forefinger, smile a self-satisfied smile, and then return the ticket to his pocket.

After he had done this some twenty times in a couple of hours, one of his fellow passengers made bold to get up and ask him what was going on.

'*Aj* railway *walayaan da ullu bana ditta e* (today I've made a complete fool of the railway fellows),' he said with a gleeful smile, with the air of one who has just given the slip to the guards at Guantanamo or San Quentin.

'How?' asked the other.

---

[5]From the film *Do Jasoos*. Meaning: Two sleuths come to realize that the world's a pretty bad place. Who's real, who's fake, everyone has a mask on his face!

'I bought a return ticket,' he explained triumphantly, 'but I'm not going to return!'

Commentary

Funny, except this isn't all fiction. It is the story of a familiar milieu where so many individuals feel the acme of smartness is in hoodwinking the system, even when the long-term harm to one's own wellbeing from such behavior is quite self-evident.

Like all great parables, this story connects the dots. To quote Emerson, 'It is one of the most beautiful compensations of this life that no man can sincerely try to help another without helping himself.' One might infer from this its converse, namely that helping oneself at the expense of others is a mug's game.

Race Singh to Conclusions

The sardar from the village was unfamiliar with the concept of a running race. On a visit to the city he chanced upon the marathon, when he suddenly saw hundreds of people dashing down the road for no apparent reason. He asked his friend what was going on. The friend explained the concept of a race, and the incentives. He said the top three finishers would get gold, silver and bronze medals respectively.

'But then ...' asked the sardar, 'why are all the others running?'

Commentary

Why indeed?

The odds of winning a lottery are miniscule, yet millions of people buy tickets religiously. The joke also highlights the stupidity of competition (life corroding competition, as Gandhi called it). It calls into question the multitude of races one participates in all through life, unwitting and witting: with classmates, siblings, colleagues, spouse, even children. The moment you leave the race, you realize the absurdity of it – the ab-Surdity, if you must.

Chessminder Singh

In 1973, Boris Spassky, the Soviet grandmaster, was defending his championship title against Bobby Fischer, the genius maverick loner from Brooklyn, New York. It was at the height of the Cold War – the prestige of superpowers was pegged on the encounter. Propaganda from both sides was incessant, and the world was soon riveted by a game normally relegated to a corner of an inside page in the newspaper.

Our story begins a few months before the meet. The Russians find that Spassky is far from his peak form. After running several tests and studies, they discover that his problem is entirely psychological. He is highly-strung, nervous and apprehensive about the coming match. Part of this, they conclude, is owing to his off the charts IQ (180 or thereabouts), which causes this instability. He is thus unable to take the pressure and is therefore distracted from his practice.

The solution, they suggest, is to bring down his IQ to somewhere around 140, and let it rise naturally back to 180 around the time of the match, which would enable him to attend to his practice and still be on top of his game at the time of his contest with Fischer.

So they admit him to the best sanatorium in the land, hooking him up with electrodes stuck to his skull, and an IQ meter to track the current level. After setting everything up, as the champion is sedated and asleep, they depute an attendant, a young fellow called Igor, to be with him at all times, to watch the IQ meter, and to alert the doctors and other senior personnel when it drops to 145.

The process is woefully slow, the attendant soon discovers. By the end of two hours the IQ meter has registered a mere two-point drop. The way this is crawling, he decides, there's plenty of time to run down to the canteen for a quick snack. He checks to see if his charge is doing okay. Spassky seems to be sleeping peacefully and dreaming happy dreams. Nothing untoward at all.

Igor leaves for the cafeteria. There he meets a couple of other youths. The discussion turns to football, and before they know it an hour has gone by. Igor heads back to the room, expecting the IQ to have dropped to perhaps 170 ...

Secrecy was the hallmark of Soviet life, and they had omitted to tell young Igor a simple fact about the machine – initially slow, the drop accelerated as time progressed.

What confronts him is a picture of his ruin. For Spassky's IQ is at 60 – and dropping. Though shocked, Igor has enough presence of mind to shut off the machine immediately. Before calling the superiors, it occurs to him that he should check if Spassky is otherwise okay. He shakes up the sleeping figure. 'Comrade, Comrade Spassky ...' he pleads. 'Wake up, please.'

The sleeping figure stirs, squints with irritation, and says in a language unintelligible to Igor, '*Oye* ^&%$^, *main kithe haan oye* (hey, where the ^&%$^ am I)?'

Commentary

This is clearly an ethnic/cultural joke used to poke fun at numerous groups by substituting the appropriate phrase at the end. As such, it may not quite qualify as an original sardar joke. Still, it does have a few instructive points to offer, first among these the folly of leaving a national treasure like Spassky in the care of an adolescent who can get sucked into a football discussion and neglect his charge. One would assume the Russians would have more sense than that, but the propensity to spend millions on trivia at one end and try to economize on vital expenses elsewhere is a universal phenomenon, commented upon several times by C Northcote Parkinson among other experts on management science.

Even more interesting is the notion that IQ can be reduced or increased using a machine, which raises a philosophical question all its own – can an individual altered suddenly in this manner still be called the same person? If Spassky could be turned into a sardar, could a sardar become a Spassky? Such transformations are the subject of the next joke.

Reversingh

From several decades ago.

Banta Singh, on a business trip to America, came across a vending machine for the first time. Not just any vending machine, but one at a Midwestern meatpacking plant. Its unique feature was that if you pressed a button, a chicken would get slaughtered, stripped, and cooked and the dish served fresh to the person using the machine. After examining the machine from all sides, Banta Singh gobsmacked his hosts by asking whether, if he wanted to return the dish, it would all go in reverse and reconstitute the live chicken once more.

Commentary

One of the great philosophical jokes. Reversibility is the biggest architectural principle of all. Any good design should have the least number of things cast in stone. All else should be reversible. We often confuse substitutability – being able to use one thing in place of another – for reversibility, but they are not the same. Substitutability is the first step on the road to loss of individuality.

If he had merely asked whether he could get his money back from the machine the hosts would probably have said yes. Or ask for a different dish, or a different plate of the same dish. But none of those things is reversibility.

The famous story of Devadatta and Siddhartha (the future Buddha) asks exactly this question: whether Devadatta who shot down the swan with his arrow could bring it back to health. Reversible processes are much more powerful (and benign, generally) than irreversible ones.

A parallel question is asked in computer science – should something be done in hardware or in software? Hardware decisions are less reversible than software decisions. On the other hand, hardware brings greater speed than software. This brings forth another question, how important is speed? Mahatma Gandhi is often quoted as saying, 'There is more to life than increasing its speed.'

Is it any good going fast (and irreversibly) in the wrong direction?

To Catch a Thief

The story goes that the famous sprinter Milkha Singh was resting one night after an intensive running practice. He was suddenly woken up by a noise from downstairs. As he put on his nightgown and descended the stairs he saw the window open, with a stranger going about the room, picking up stuff calmly and putting it into a bag. Milkha Singh yelled, 'Oye, kaun hai oye.' Upon this the thief made a rapid exit, jumping out through the open window. Milkha followed, and by the time he was out, he could spot the thief already at the far end of the street. Naturally, he set off in hot pursuit. Milkha was surprised at the thief's abilities, for he gave him a good run.

Not for long, though.

A champ is a champ, after all. Although handicapped by being barefoot and in his pajamas, he did it. It took a special

effort on his part but by the end of hundred yards, Milkha Singh had overtaken the thief.

Commentary

We are so stuck in our ways that even when the circumstances change, we continue doing what we are used to. The mind is a dumb machine, unwilling to shift gears and unable to do so easily, beholden to inertia. Here instead of catching the thief, the sprinter, true to his habit, overtook him.

Another thief vs Milkha encounter follows.

A Sandal in Bohemia

Given what had happened that night Milkha Singh found it hard to sleep the following night. His friends had given him no end of ribbing for overtaking the thief instead of catching him. He was determined, should the chance present itself, not let such a thing happen again. He even slept in his running shoes and tracksuit to be on the ready for any such contingency.

Sure enough, he was awakened once again by noises from below. This time he crept softly downstairs, hoping to catch the thief red handed. Unfortunately, he stepped on a tray of golf balls and made an unexpectedly loud landing. The thief – who had been hoping to complete the unfinished job from the previous night – lost no time in making good his escape. This time Milkha was better equipped: tracksuit and running shoes, remember? He leaped through the window and was able to catch up with the thief in a few minutes. And this time he actually caught – not overtook – the thief.

After cuffing him a few times and letting fly some choice words, Milkha said, 'Let's go to the police station, you scoundrel.'

'I beg you, sir,' said the thief. 'I took off my sandals at your house so as to make no noise.' Milkha looked down and saw this was true enough. The thief was indeed barefoot.

'Go and fetch them quickly. I'll be waiting right here,' he ordered.

That was the last he saw of the thief, until ...

Next night.

After this incident his friends had been unsparing in their ridicule. 'You what!! Sent him off to fetch his chappals? Hey guys, listen to this ...!'

Actually, not only had the thief gone off, he had even gone in and collected his chappals before he left. Milkha was determined that this would not happen again. It didn't – at least, not in the same way.

The next night, the same drill. Milkha was again prepared. There was a noise, the thief stepped in, Milkha was right there, the thief escaped and ran, Milkha chased and caught hold of him. The thief tried the same trick. 'Sahib, my chappals are still at your house.'

Milkha had anticipated this. 'You think I'm going to fall for that again?' he thundered, giving the boy a clip on the ear for good measure. '^&%$^, you've already shown you can't be trusted.'

After pondering a little, Milkha told the thief, 'You wait right here. I'll go and get the chappals!'

Commentary

I think we've milk(ha)'d this joke enough. Suffice it to say that we are often apt to learn lessons in pieces, painfully even, and not draw the complete conclusion as we ought to. Part of it is laziness, a reluctance to work through the thought process. 'There is no expedient to which a man will not go to avoid the labor of thinking,' as Thomas Edison is reputed to have said.

Absence of Proof is Not Proof of Absence

Whatever its repute within the country, the intellectual acumen of sardars has done India proud at numerous world forums, and remains unsurpassed at least in the realm of jokes.

At an archaeological conference two professors from France got up to present for the first time some revolutionary findings from their excavations in Turkey.

'We found what looks like telephone wires, at a depth of forty feet,' exulted one of them. 'Clearly Asia Minor was using – or close to using – electrical communications as early as the second century AD!' A rapt audience gasped in amazement at their color pictures.

Next came India's turn. Professor Banta Singh spoke. 'I have listened with great interest to the French professors' presentation,' he began. 'I was particularly interested because in our Kapurthala district we also conducted extensive excavations. We dug and dug, up to hundred feet.'

Pictures of a big crater appeared on the screen with nothing but cranes and earth movers. The audience held its breath for some major revelation.

Professor Banta continued. 'No wires were found.'

As the audience's enthusiasm deflated he declared, 'Obviously we Indians were using cell phones and wireless technology even in the BC era.'

Commentary

Despite the superficial idiocy of the statement, Dr Banta Singh is on to a very important discovery here. Absence is frequently just as significant as presence, a fact illustrated best in the Sherlock Holmes' short story, *Silver Blaze* (paraphrased below):

'I commend your attention to the curious behavior of the dog in the night.'

'But the dog did nothing in the night.'

'That was the curious incident.'

The entire basis of semiconductor physics is dependent on the concept of 'hole' which stands for the absence of an electron.

Shunyata (emptiness) is a central concept in Hindu philosophy. Everything arises from Nothing.

The philosopher/mathematician/anti-nuclear activist Bertrand Russell once told the visiting Indian iconoclast and scholar Nirad Chaudhuri, 'You Indians invented nothing!' Initially, Chaudhuri attributed the remark to Russell's brusque manner and low view of India, detecting in it perhaps an echo of his own notions. Only later did he realize that Russell was praising India for providing one of the greatest inventions of the human race – the concept of Zero.

The Lesser Evil

Sardarji had gotten into a serious accident. Fortunately, he had survived, but was laid up for a few weeks. His colleagues learned of his mishap the following day at work, and decided to pay him a visit after the office closed.

Seeing him in an ocean of bandages, they did not know what commiseration to offer. 'Well, at least you're alive' seemed too generic, not to say cold. Finally, one of them noticed a silver lining. He managed, 'Sardarji, you are lucky it is only the left hand that's hurt. How fortunate it wasn't the right hand. That would have made it really difficult.'

The hitherto crestfallen sardarji brightened suddenly at this remark. 'Thank you, ji. Thank you. You are the first one to notice,' he said. 'You see, I too thought the same thing. Actually it was my right hand that was about to get hit. Fortunately, I have good reflexes. I quickly removed it and placed my left hand instead.'

Commentary

Don't think it is so outlandish. The world is full of people making such false decisions everyday: getting a daughter married off to one bad guy over another because the dowry was a little less, or paying more dowry because the groom was a little less worse.

I recall a heart patient in Delhi in an adjoining hospital bed many years ago. When the doctors were away he would have a buddy sneak in a pack of cigarettes. The doctors learned of it and urged him to quit. He explained that he had upped his brand to a costlier one, and when the new federal budget raised taxes and put prices beyond his reach, he would be constrained to quit smoking. I relayed this to my visiting uncle, also a smoker. He chuckled, 'When the price goes up he'll simply come back to his old brand. It's all that's going to happen.' The 'lesser evil' philosophy forgets that the lesser evil is evil too. But it is often touted as the pragmatic way to live, and the deep roots of this conventional wisdom are the despair of many an Indian idealist and social reformer.

Mirth Control

Then there was another international conference; this one on family planning. Delegates from various countries presented the inventions they had made in this field, and animated discussions followed.

Finally, it was India's turn. Professor Banta Singh rose and said, 'Ladies and gentlemen, we in India have discovered that there is no need for elaborate birth control devices, surgeries minor or major, or even medication, for family planning ...

'We have discovered that drinking a glass of water will do the trick!'

A hushed silence fell upon the gathering, followed by thunderous applause. Then several dozen hands went up simultaneously among the audience, and when the speaker called on one of them, the delegate echoed the question that was on everyone's mind:

'Before or after, Dr Banta?' he asked.

'Instead,' replied Banta Singh.

Commentary

The beautiful simplicity here is reminiscent of the ideas of Tolstoy or Gandhi.

This was, in fact, Gandhi's recommended method of birth control, abstinence.

Ronald Reagan once said that many things have a simple solution, but not necessarily an easy one. Or, as Miyagi noted in one of *The Karate Kid* movies, the best solution to a fight is to not be there. Alexander's Gordian Knot is the finest example of thinking outside the box, so to say.

The Uprisingh

The French Revolution was in full fury, with the mob baying for blood. Unfortunately for them, three young men were caught one morning on suspicion of aiding the nobility: an American, a German, and a sardar.

One by one, they were led to the *guillotine*.

The American was asked, 'What is your final wish?' He replied that he would like to smoke a cigar. He was allowed to do so. When he was finished, he was led to the guillotine, and his neck placed on the chopping block. The blade was released.

He heard a 'swish' as it descended, but was surprised to find himself alive a few seconds later. The blade had stopped a few inches above his neck!

The mob's policy was that once the blade was dropped the execution was done. If someone didn't die, that was that. The American was told he should thank his lucky stars, and get out of France ASAP. He hurried away.

Next came the German's turn. He asked for some beer and sausage, and it was brought. Upon finishing his meal he was taken to the guillotine. And once more the blade stopped short of the neck by a few centimeters. The crowd howled in disappointment, but they were bound by the rules. The German was also asked to leave the country.

Finally, it was the sardar's turn. When asked what he would like for his last wish, he expressed a yearning for a super-combo of *makki-di-roti* and *sarson-da-saag*,[6] to be washed down with some *meethi lassi*.[7] When this was all conveyed to the executioners, in broken translation, a huddle followed. After some deliberation they expressed to the sardar their regrets at their inability to provide the same. Probably a genuine impossibility in revolutionary Paris.

---

[6]*Makki-di-roti* is a flatbread made of maize. *Sarson-da-saag* is made from mustard leaves. Together the two are a delicious favorite in rural Punjab.
[7]Sweet buttermilk.

But sardarji was indignant. A promise is a promise, he said, unwittingly taking his cue from Shylock. An argument ensued. Words flew, tempers rose.

Finally the sardar said to the leader of the mob, '*Vadda bol rea ai toon*. Machine *ta^&%$^ chaldi nahin teri* ... (is there nothing you guys can do right? First of all, this ^&%$^ machine of yours doesn't even work ...)'

Commentary

Truth, said Mark Twain, is a valuable commodity and should be employed sparingly. Not everything that is true need be spelled out. Not everything need be said everyplace.

Discrimination is a great asset, as this example shows, and getting angry is also an art. We talked of reversibility earlier, and words are among the most irreversible of all.

The temptation to prove we are right is the cause of many a downfall. It wasn't for nothing that the old line in business went, 'the customer is always right'.

Above all, the joke shouts out the wisdom of silence.

Testing Times

A friend was selling his car and wanted to make sure all the signals were OK before he placed an ad in the paper. He requested Banta Singh to stand outside and let him know if the various lights functioned properly as he turned them on and off. Banta agreed readily.

They began with the front lights. The friend turned them on.

'Working,' said Banta, pointing his thumbs up.

Then the friend asked him to check out the rear lights.

'Working,' said Banta, thumbs up once more to his friend watching the rear-view mirror.

Then the brake lights, front and rear. 'Working' came the answer, with a thumbs-up again.

It was now time to check the turn signals. The friend put on the right turn indicator. 'See now,' he said to Banta.

'Working, not working, working, not working, working, not working ...' was the reply from outside, accompanied by oscillating thumbs up and down signs.

Commentary

A story with a very great moral. It is folly to think that everything is – or ought to be – monotonic (one-directional). In fact, many a process in life consists of this seesaw, for the lack of which the process would be incomplete. A turn indicator to work properly needs both the ON and OFF states.

As Kahlil Gibran says, 'The deeper that sorrow carves into your being, the more joy you can contain.' Opposites alone give meaning to each other, and thus form the basis for experience.

The Bhagavad Gita's injunction to transcend opposites is not to deny them but to see them both as integral parts of the same process. This joke is a perfect illustration of that idea.

Dilli Door Ast

Many years ago, a sardar was traveling from Madras to New Delhi by train. He had a transistor radio, and would try to catch whichever stations he could along the way to get some music and some news. Everyone else in the compartment knew he was going to Delhi, for he had spoken about how it was his first visit to the city and how much he was looking forward to it. They were, therefore, surprised to see him suddenly gather his luggage and get down at Mathura[8] station, the stop before Delhi. They thought he had changed his mind.

After the train had left, sardarji discovered that he had disembarked at Mathura instead of Delhi. He protested that the radio had misinformed him. Had it not proclaimed just a few minutes ago, 'Yeh Dilli hai'[9]!

Commentary

The radio had made its station identification by saying, 'This is Delhi.' The sardarji took it to mean that the train had reached Delhi. Why should the radio know anything about where the train was heading?

But the mind is a monomaniac. It seldom questions its own assumptions and presumptions, as is shown by this true story. Many

---

[8]An ancient city not far from New Delhi, reputedly the birthplace of the Hindu deity, Lord Krishna.
[9]'This is Delhi' – the standard station identification signature for All India Radio's Delhi station.

years ago, a freshly arrived Indian student in America went out one evening with an Indian friend who had been a year longer in the States. They went to have a cup of coffee at a restaurant.

The time was about 8:30 in the evening, and the senior friend, who loved his fun and wanted to take advantage of the newcomer's infatuation with all things American, had a sudden brainwave. He said to his friend, 'Arre dekh, itni advanced technology hai yahan pe (you know, here technology is so advanced). The machine outside gives you up-to-the-minute value of the dollar in rupees.' (In those days it was around rupees 8.40 to the dollar).

The freshman could barely contain his excitement. Every few minutes he would pop out and look at the large digital clock outside and proclaim how the rupee had fallen so sharply.

By the time they left the restaurant the 'exchange rate' had gone up by a full rupee. Our friend's animation was now beyond control. When he returned to the apartment he told all his friends from India news of the latest rate, before his friend informed him gently that the joke was on him.

We never ceased to rib him about it subsequently, but he was a reasonably bright guy, a graduate of IIT Bombay if memory serves right. Why did he fall for such an obvious trick? So overwhelmed was he by the American mystique that it never occurred to him to ask why one particular currency should be featured in front of any restaurant, particularly one in some remote college town. The answer is: mind-lock. In the past few days, just prior to coming to America, his mind was full of what things would cost, in rupees and dollars, and this mindset continued to dominate his thoughts, leading him to think his problems were exercising the whole world.

Changé-Changé or Change-Change?

Sardar Banta Singh was a successful businessman in Delhi. But first and foremost he was a dutiful son, who would send three hundred rupees without fail to his aged mother in his village, by money order on the tenth of each month.

His mother, though not formally educated, was literate enough to write a basic letter. She could read only slowly and with effort, however, because of her rudimentary knowledge and her cataract. Somehow she managed to compose a letter to her son, saying,

Pyaare puttar Bantaya,[10]

I am so happy that you are such a good son, and send me money so promptly each month. Your mother's blessing will always be upon you. But I have one request, puttar. The postman here only gives me the money in hundred and fifty rupee notes, and no one in the village has change for such big notes. Could you send me the money in smaller change?

May you live long and prosper.
Jeet Kaur

Banta Singh read the letter with great care and emotion. Picking out a sheet, he wrote very, very slowly,

---

[10]Dear Banta, my son.

32

Poojya Ma-ji,[11]

I am writing this letter very slowly because I know you cannot read fast.
From now on I will send the money in small change.
I would have sent some money with this letter but I have already sealed the envelope.

Pranams,

Your obedient son,
Banta

True to his word, the very next morning he went to the *Gol Dak Khana*[12] in Delhi carrying three hundred rupees in denominations of five, one, and quarter rupee coins!

Commentary

Here Banta Singh errs on several levels.

One, reciprocity does not necessarily mean symmetry – how slow something is written has no bearing on how fast it may be read.

Second, he forgets that the commodity transported by money order is not money but information.

On a deeper level the story illustrates the perils of ignoring a fundamental principle of communication: it is dangerous to assume something we say to be received by the other party in the same sense as we meant. What one says and what the other hears are two separate and often entirely disparate things, as any married person can attest!

---

[11]Revered mother.
[12]Literally, Circular Post Office, a New Delhi landmark.

Distance No Bar

Skipping over the one where the sardar goes to sleep wearing his reading glasses so as to be able to dream more clearly, we come to the Eiffel Tower visit, where Santa and Banta Singh get separated in the crowd. Soon Santa is up in the tower, and he finds that Banta is nowhere to be seen. He is quite visibly agitated and worried; this was before the age of the cell phone. Finally, a fellow tourist suggests he borrow his binoculars to scan for his friend in the crowd.

Santa looks through the binoculars and spots Banta, still on the ground looking for him. He yells out for him, but he is too far away. He is almost a speck. Then Santa has a brainwave. Looking through the binoculars again, where Banta is his normal size, he whispers, *'Oye Banteya, main itthe haan* (oye Banta, here I am).'

Commentary

Obviously no one would do that, but the general point is still quite valid. A uni-dimensional preoccupation makes us ignore or exclude seemingly extraneous information.

The other issue here is of transference. We tend to transfer one line of reasoning to others. Experience and inference aren't always readily movable, though we fancy they can be.

A Leap of Faith

A sardar was standing on the balcony of his eighth floor apartment one summer evening, enjoying the view. Suddenly someone shouted from the next building, 'Oye Banta Singh, I just saw your daughter Preeto. She said she was eloping with her boyfriend and they were off to get married.' Since the neighbor was shouting this across the open courtyard, other residents also heard him, and were looking at him and the sardar from their balconies.

Unable to bear this very public ignominy, the sardar flung himself off the balcony. The neighbors gave a collective gasp of horror at what they were watching.

As he passed the sixth floor he thought to himself, 'I don't have a daughter called Preeto.'

As he passed the fourth floor he remembered that he was a bachelor and did not even have a wife, let alone children.

As he passed the second floor something else occurred to him: 'My name isn't Banta Singh.'

Commentary

I think this joke provides two meaningful insights. One, so many people spend their entire lives engaged in battles and consumed by issues that really have very little to do with them. Secondly, our realizations grow as we get closer to the end of our lives, even as our ability to do anything about them grows in inverse proportion to the wisdom we have garnered.

State Bank of Bikaner & Jaipur

The group of revelers was raucous and rowdy, even if they meant no harm. They were all very drunk, having just ushered in the New Year at a Connaught Place[13] restaurant. Few of them were in any condition to walk, let alone drive. As such they were a natural fodder for the police patrol car cruising the streets in search of exactly this category of offenders on this particular night.

The police car pulled up next to them, and a couple of hefty Haryanvi[14] cops jumped out.

Pulling out a notebook, they shook each of the youths and asked for their names. The first guy was alert enough not to give his real name. But as happens when we are pressed, he couldn't think of a plausible false name. For a moment his mind went blank. Then he recovered smartly, and quickly surveying the shops around him, read out, 'SC Sharma' from one of the signboards.

The second guy caught on, and when asked, said, 'D Vaish,' from another shop signboard. The others in the group took up the cue, and so it continued, one signboard after another.

The two rustic cops dutifully wrote the names down, and clearly had no idea they were being tricked.

Meanwhile the sardar too had figured out the game plan. By the time his turn came he knew exactly what he was going to say.

---

[13]New Delhi's marquee downtown and shopping district.
[14]From the nearby state of Haryana.

'And, sardarji, your name?' asked the cop.

Pat came the reply with a confident toss of the head, 'The State Bank of Bikaner and Jaipur.'

Commentary

It is entirely possible that the cops duly noted down the sardar's answer too, and moved on without suspecting anything. Cops are as mechanical in their ways as the rest of us, and in any case, nimbleness of intellect is hardly the first attribute that springs to mind when thinking of the Delhi police.

It also goes to show it is possible to belong and even thrive in a group without grasping anything about what is going on around oneself.

Arms and the Man

Sardar Baldev Singh was India's first defense minister, and the central figure in a whole legion of sardar jokes. In many of these, Prime Minister Jawaharlal Nehru too figures as a straight man.[15]

My favorite Baldev Singh joke starts at a Nehru press conference in London. Baldev Singh is also present. In some context, in a serious tone, Nehru lets drop a revelation.

---

[15]From Webster: A member of a comedy team who feeds lines to a partner who in turn replies with usually humorous quips.

'As for me,' he says with a wistful smile, 'some of the happiest hours of my life were spent in the arms of another man's wife.'

A collective gasp escapes the room as even the most hard-bitten journalists jerk to attention.

Adds Nehru, slowly. 'I am referring, of course, to my mother.' The laughter and cheers last a full two minutes.

Baldev Singh is determined to learn by watching Nehru's masterful ways with the foreign press. Back in India at his next news conference, he repeats Nehru's words, in as serious tone as he had seen Nehru do.

'Well, the happiest hours of my life were spent in the arms of another man's wife,' he says.

There is a stunned silence. The Indian press is flabbergasted. What a scandal! This would rock the country.

'Who? Who? Who was the lady?' everyone shouts.

Sardar Baldev Singh waits for the hubbub to settle before delivering the punch line. 'Nehru's mother,' he concludes, with a smile.

Commentary

This goes to show the dangers of incomplete understanding. Knowing the external symbols without comprehending what is going on under the covers can lead to some nasty surprises.

Back in college a girl who used to travel with us wanted to know the trick to get down from a running bus, as she had seen so many boys do. One of our friends kindly educated her, telling her how she should lean back as she stepped off the bus. The next day she was complaining of bruises after having fallen down while trying his method. On closer examination it turned out she had leaned *back* when the bus was *reversing*, a very bad idea indeed. She was lucky she wasn't hurt badly!

The Common Factor

A teetotaler all his life, Banta Singh decided to give the social circuit a try. Each day he would go out to a pub to have a different drink. One day he had whisky and soda, the next day rum and soda, the third day vodka and soda, and so on.

By the week's end he found he had hangovers every single time. He concluded this was not for him, and decided to give up soda.

Commentary

The pitfall of the obvious is real. As Isaac Asimov wrote, any fool could see the sun went round the earth!

Bayan Hatth Da Khed (Child's Play)

On a long flight from the US to India, sardarji found himself sitting in the executive section of the plane next to a distinguished passenger – Gary Kasparov, the international grandmaster.

The two nodded and smiled at each other but that was it. An hour into the flight, when sardarji woke up from his nap, Kasparov smiled again, then pulled out a small chess set and asked sardarji if he would like to play a sporting game of chess - $100 a game.

Sardarji smiled. 'My dear Mr Kasparov, don't you think I know who you are? As for wagering on games with you, I have already spent far too much for this first-class ticket and I have no desire to lose any more money.'

Kasparov smiled too. 'You are a smart cookie, Mr Singh. I should have known better. Still it would be a pity to waste all this time on the plane. Hmmm .... how 'bout this ... I'll give you a little advantage. How about if I play with my left hand?' he asked. 'That should even things up a little.'

Sardarji thought about it and decided this was reasonable. The games proved intense because sardarji thought long and hard before making his moves. It did not improve his prospects, but at least it reduced the number of games, saving him some money. Suffice it to say that, by the time they arrived in New Delhi, he was some $800 in the red. Fortunately he could afford the loss, and after all, how many people could boast they had played so many games with Gary Kasparov?

When he reached Amritsar that evening, he could hardly wait to relate the whole incident to his bosom friend Banta Singh. 'Oye Banteya,' he lamented after finishing his tale. 'Even with his left hand, he just demolished me, *praavaa*.'

Banta Singh listened silently to the entire story, fascinated, and then slowly shook his head in pity. '*Oye khottaya*,'[16] he

---

[16]Punjabi for ass or donkey.

chided his friend gently, 'you may be a big businessman now, but you have remained the simpleton you always were. You fall for such old tricks. I could see through this fellow's plans right away ...'

'Obviously this Kasparov must be a *khabbu* (left-hander)!' continued Banta Singh.

Commentary

One more example of missing the inner truth for the outer. The adage goes, 'Don't judge a book by its cover.' Unfortunately, in our packaging age we are often attracted or repelled by the outer appearance. In any decision it is essential to recognize what is incidental and what is central to the issue. Aristotle called these two factors the 'essential' and 'accidental' elements of a problem.

The Sun Singh

At an elite antique store in Paris, a multi-millionaire sardar is looking for a suitable bed to furnish the restored château he had purchased in the outskirts.

He tries out various beds, and finds that he likes the Louis XIV style best. But he is a tall man, and finds the bed perfect for his taste except that it is a shade too short for him. He makes some quick mental calculations, then calls out to an attendant.

'Excusez moi, madame,' he says with a bow to the saleslady who is showing him around the boutique. 'Please pack for me a Louis XVII bed.'

Commentary

It is an invaluable skill to be able to transfer truths and interrelationships across contexts. This example illustrates that such transferability cannot be assumed. Sometimes, as here, one set of measurements has nothing to do with another. There is no connection. Sometimes, they may be related inversely. At other times, the connection may be quite convoluted.

For example, in a cricket match a high score is good, not so in a golf game. However, this kind of correlation is often made when the mind is on auto-pilot. Obviously there is no rule that each French king had to be taller than his predecessor. But our mind seeks to economize on the information it needs to store, and thus the sardar's error in this case.

A minor matter, but there was no Louis XVII. The French Revolution did away with Louis XVI, and that was the end of the monarchy in France.

Recognisingh

Question: How can you tell who is Banta Singh in a classroom?

Answer: He's the one who's erasing his notebook whenever the teacher erases the board.

Commentary

We seek to reduce tasks to automatic mode. This of course is an extreme example, but how easy it would be for Banta Singh to copy the teacher's every step, including erasure! The mind would be entirely taken out of the equation.

The Age of Science

The sardar was stretched out on the upper berth of a train that had just left New Delhi station. His eye caught that of the lower berth passenger and they exchanged a smile; passengers saying hello to fellow passengers is the normal course of interaction on Indian trains.

Slowly the inevitable question came up. 'Where are you heading?' the sardar asked the other.

'To Bombay,' came the reply.

Sardarji shook his head in wonder. '*Yaar* science *di tarakki vi k'maal hai* (wondrous is the progress of science). Lower berth going to Bombay, upper berth going to Amritsar! *Wah Wah. Kya baat hai!*'

He was on the wrong train.

Commentary

We start by assuming we are right. The general human tendency is to reduce what needs to be changed, or to eliminate it completely.

The laziness of the body is nothing compared with that of the mind. And the mind has the luxury of constructing its own realities and believing in them, so it can even pretend (for a while at least) that black is white and night is day.

Dr John Sarno of New York has written several books about how our own brain can create physical ailments in order to divert our attention from unbearable (to the conscious) happenings in our lives.

In this instance, it would have been excruciating for the sardar to consider the possibility of being on the wrong train.

Of course, there is also the opposite state of mind, where someone may doubt themselves so much that they think they are wrong even when they are right. For example, what if the fellow on the lower berth was wrong, and the train was indeed going to Amritsar?

One would agree that both impulses are essential. We do need a degree of confidence so as not to be swayed by every opinion expressed to us. We also need to be alert to the possibility that we may be wrong, and hence willing to change should that be so. A description of the ideal balance is given by Kipling:

> *If you can keep your head when all around you,*
> > *Are losing theirs and blaming it on you,*
> *If you can trust yourself when all men doubt you*
> > *But make allowance for their doubting too ...*

I read somewhere that Kipling's *If*, from where these lines are quoted, was Mahatma Gandhi's favorite poem.

The Common Factor Again

'What is the similarity between Rama, Krishna, Jesus, Mohammed, Nanak, Buddha, Mahavira and Mahatma Gandhi?' asked the teacher.

'They were all born on government holidays,' replied Banta Singh.

Commentary

Banta Singh is actually on excellent ground here. After all, to most people, it is safe to say, a holiday is a holiday is a holiday. The only reason Banta Singh knows some of the names in that list is because of the public holiday against their birthday.

It is also an excellent warning against megalomania: *To scatter plenty o'er a smiling land/And read their history in a nation's eyes*, to quote Gray's Elegy, of dreaming of being remembered. It tells us that even the greatest figures fade away over time except for completely trivial reasons having nothing to do with their deeds. The same Gray's Elegy cautions,

> *The Boast of Heraldry,*
> *The Pomp of Power*
> *And all the Beauty that Wealth e'er gave*
> *Awaits alike the inevitable hour*
> *The paths of glory lead but to the grave.*

Banta Singh is merely telling us the same thing in plain prose.

Identity Crisis

It was 1:15 a.m. when sardarji's train reached Pathankot Junction. He had to catch another train to Kangra at 4:30 a.m., and he was dog-tired. The railway waiting room seemed completely full. His eyes were drooping even as he spoke to the porter. '*Sun kaka* (listen, my dear fellow),' he said. 'I will be generous and give you twenty rupees right now. I am going to sleep on the platform. You need to get me on the Kangra train at 4:30, whether I'm awake or asleep. OK? Here is my compartment and berth number. I'm trusting you. If you fail me you will go to hell.'

'No problem, sirjee,'[17] said the porter. And true to his word, he somehow managed to get the sardar not only on the train but even on the right berth. When he left, the sardar's luggage was all stacked neatly and he was fast asleep on his berth, without being aware of his being helped on to the train, etc.

Around 5:30 a.m. a barber got on at a minor stop, and was making his rounds asking if anyone wanted an early morning shave. Sardarji had his turban off, and perhaps nodded in his sleep. Anyhow, the barber gave him a shave, collected a couple of rupees from the drowsy figure, and moved on.

---

[17]A word that combines the English 'sir' and the Hindi 'ji' or 'jee' (both meaning 'sir'). Beginning in North Indian government schools in the 1960s, it gained wider currency in the late 1980s and is now commonly used in North India while addressing superiors, and generally while addressing elders.

Around 8 a.m. as the train pulled into Jwalamukhi Road, sardarji got up to go and have a wash. In the bathroom he stared at the mirror for a while, and returned to his compartment, furious and full of rich oaths.

His fellow passengers enquired what the problem was.

'Damn coolies!' was his reply, followed by a smorgasbord of Punjabi's finest *gaalis*.

'But at least tell us what happened,' they insisted.

Finally, he calmed down enough to explain what was upsetting him, 'The son-of-a-bitch took twenty rupees from me but put someone else on the train!' he thundered.

Commentary

Note the words. '... put *someone else* on the train!'

Here the sardar is taking on the central question in Advaita: Who am I?

It's understandable that a person who has never shaved his face is likely to associate himself with his beard and mustache, and that it will take some time for him to get used to associating himself with a different face.

We laugh at this joke because it is obvious to us that he is the same person. But is it not also true that we look at ourselves differently depending on what has happened to us during the day? After all, are we not the same people regardless of whether the day went well or badly?

The joke also casts some light upon the importance we attach to the outer appearance. Nor is this wrong, because in a world where everybody goes by the outer appearance, it is hardly to be ignored.

If you take the premise of the sardar joke (not just this one) to be that the world is an absurd place and that public opinion is so entirely contrived as to have no meaning by itself, the philosophy of this joke comes through loud and clear.

Kidnapped!

During the ten years of mayhem in Punjab in the late 1980s and early 90s, it was common to find sons of rich industrialists being kidnapped and held for ransom by pro-Khalistan groups. It is a tactic common to many rebel groups including the LTTE and more recently the Maoists in Jharkhand and Chhattisgarh.

The story goes that a rebel group of sardars had kidnapped the twelve-year old son of the noted industrialist and philanthropist, Sardar Banta Singh.

After letting the family stew in fear and desperation for a few days, the rebel leader writes a ransom note, a short and crisp affair:

If you don't pay us ₹100,000 by nightfall tomorrow you will only see your son's coffin.
PS: Don't try any tricks like going to the police.

Sealing the envelope, he beckons the kidnapped boy and says to him, 'Take this to your father.'

The boy leaves.

The following day Banta Singh sends the money to the rebel leader – delivered by his son.

Commentary

While this sequence is laughably absurd, it is actually not at all unknown in negotiation. There is sometimes no greater bond than that which gets formed between erstwhile enemies. The rebel leader's gesture may be interpreted as another sardar joke, or it might be viewed as a grand gesture. Banta Singh's reciprocation when he had no need to do so is also an interesting way to build a trust which makes any future depredation by this rebel group more difficult to justify in their own minds.

All at Sea

Shortly after Indian Independence, in September 1947 to be precise, Pakistani irregulars were breaking into Kashmir. Indian Prime Minister Nehru and his colleague Vallabhbhai Patel were agonizing over what to do. There were army divisions to be mobilized. The air force was going to have to undertake non-stop drops of supplies and men.

To Sardar Baldev Singh, the defense minister, it seemed a terrible waste to ignore a proud branch of the armed forces at such an important juncture.

He ventured a thought, 'Why not send the navy to Kashmir?[18]'

---

[18]Kashmir is land-locked.

Commentary

In a crisis we have a tendency to call up all the resources at our command, even if we do not have any current use for some of them. Often this is just a mental justification on our part. We cannot tolerate it that some are working hard while others are not. Sometimes an organization's structure is altered just to face a crisis. Perhaps in this case it was even justified to have navy personnel working alongside the other armed forces till the crisis was tided over. So, even if the episode is true, Sardar Baldev Singh's words may not be as ridiculous as they sound.

A Double Irony?

The doctor was horrified when Banta Singh showed him the burn he had sustained; the left side of his face turned toward the doctor to show the raw and red skin.

'What happened?' asked the doctor, horrified.

'Well, doctor sahib, I was ironing my shirt when the phone rang. Out of habit, I grabbed the hot iron by mistake and placed it against my ear ... and it was a wrong number,' he grimaced as he spoke.

'Oh, my God!' winced the doctor. Then he noticed that the right side of Banta Singh's face had a similar burn. 'But what happened to the other side, sardar sahib?' he asked.

'Well, the same fellow called again ...' replied Banta Singh.

Commentary

Funnily enough, this story has a long provenance, all the way back to the Mahabharata, no less.

The story of Prince Yudhisthira, a gambling aficionado, getting inveigled by his cousins and their uncle Sakuni into a crooked game of dice, is well known to most Indians. Caught up in the frenzy of the game, he pledges not only his kingdom, but his brothers and his wife Draupadi too, losing them all. His opponents take the opportunity to insult his family and even try to disrobe his wife in the middle of the royal court.

Many Indians will also remember that Yudhisthira lost his game of dice and had to go into exile along with his brothers and wife for twelve years as a result.

What many might not remember, if they didn't pay attention, was that this was the *second* time Yudhisthira had lost the game of dice.

So here's the deal: a mythological hero, an exemplar of good judgment, the epitome of truth, a man known for deliberating long and hard about Dharma[19] before taking each step, Dharmaputra (as Yudhisthira was also known), could fall prey to making the same mistake twice in rapid succession. And not just some trivial mistake – these were momentous decisions affecting the lives and liberty of his brothers and his wife, and the destiny of his kingdom.

Can you really fault Banta Singh all that much for absentmindedly picking up the 'phone' twice?

---

[19]Dharma: roughly translated, the rights and wrongs of a situation, and one's own moral duty therein.

Joora-Sikh Park?

Banta Singh and Bachittar Singh went to see the movie, *Jurassic Park*. As the dinosaurs came hurtling on the large screen with stereo sound effects magnifying the terror, the young ones in the audience screamed and even older people were on the edge of their seats. Banta Singh was terrified, and cowered in his chair.

'*Oye Bante, ki fiqar haegi oye* (hey Banta, what're you worried about),' said Bachittar. 'It is only a movie; relax, yaar.'

'*Oye khottaya, ae movie e woh to main vi jaanda haan te tu vi jaanda e. Magar ae cheez aus* dinosaur *nu thori pata e* (you numbskull, I know and you know that it is only a movie. But does that dinosaur know it)?' was Banta's answer.

Commentary

Despite its evident absurdity, Banta's concern is not at all wrong.

They teach a concept called 'Defensive Driving' in Drivers Ed(ucation) schools in America. This is to emphasize a very important and often forgotten point: *just because you have followed all the rules does not mean that you are immune to accidents.* After all, there are perfectly rule-abiding drivers and pedestrians who are hit by careless or drunk drivers each day. A good driver abides by the rules, of course, but good driving is more than just that. It includes the vital element of awareness, of what other drivers around you are up to, of road conditions, etc. It is taking into account potential violations of rules by others and taking evasive or other measures necessary to keep safe.

Something I came across recently says it well, 'Expecting that bad things will never happen to you because you are good is like expecting the lion will not eat you because you are vegetarian.'

The Audacity of Hope – The Original

There was a popular foreign film running at Rivoli Cinema in New Delhi's Connaught Place many years ago. The film was renowned for one scene, celebrated as particularly sensuous. It featured the hero and heroine in a suggestive embrace, holding out prospects of even more exciting happenings. Just as the audience was having its collective heartbeat aflutter, a train would go thundering across the screen, eclipsing the amorous pair. By the time the train had passed, it was all over and back to more humdrum elements of the story line. It left moviegoers enthralled, the very essence of good filmmaking from all accounts.

A sardar used to watch every showing of the movie, three times a day, every single day of the week. Now, he was not known as a student of cinematography or anything like that. But, since he duly purchased a ticket for each show no one could stop him either.

At the end of two weeks, however, the attendant at Rivoli Cinema could resist his curiosity no longer. 'Sardar sahib, *is movie mein aisi bhi kya baat hai jo aap roz roz dekhne aate hain* (sardarji, what's so special about this movie that you keep coming to watch it every day, day after day)?'

'*Oye main kehriyan*,' replied the sardar, '*ik na ik din ao sali gaddi z'roor* late *aani aan* (hey, I'm betting, one of these days that bloody train is bound to be late).'

Commentary

Perhaps this bears out the truth that 'hope springs eternal in the human breast', as the English poet wrote. But it also shows that we are often blinded to the obvious by our own cleverness.

Identity Politics, Again

The sales clerk at the appliance store stared with a somber face as the sardarji pointed to an item on the shelf and said, 'I want to buy that color tv.'

'Sorry, sir, we don't serve sardars,' the clerk whispered to him. 'Company policy. Something to do with the owner's orders.'

Sardarji was furious, and normally a fusillade of *gaalis* would have been issued forth just for starters, and the salesman and owner's ancestry made known to all the customers in the shop. But the deal was really good and he didn't want to lose it by picking a fight or complaining to the manager. So he restrained himself, and thought hard about what he could do.

The next day he discarded his turban and put on a hat and sun glasses, then approached the clerk again and, pointing at the item, said, 'How much is that color tv, please?'

To his surprise, the clerk betrayed no sign that he remembered him from yesterday but gave the same reply, with the same impassive look, 'Sorry, sir, we don't serve sardars.'

The sardarji was completely flummoxed. The objective for him now became twofold. Actually, evading detection by the clerk became even more of a priority than getting the tv, in this game between him and the clerk.

The next day he actually trimmed his beard, wore an *achkan*,[20] *chooridar*,[21] and leather chappals, put a *fez*[22] cap on his head, and donned a different pair of sunglasses. He looked a Muslim *hazrat*[23] to his fingertips. His own wife was unable to recognize him.

Convinced this would do the trick, he went to the shop and approached the clerk once again, saying, in a different voice and in Urdu, 'Janaab, I would like to buy that tv,' pointing to the shelf.

'Sorry, sir, we don't serve sardars,' said the clerk once again.

The sardar could stand the mystery no more. How could this young whippersnapper see through his costume when no one else had?

'How the hell do you know I'm a sardar?' he blurted out.

'Because, sir, that's a microwave oven, not a tv,' replied the clerk.

---

[20]A long and high-necked Indian coat.
[21]Tight-fitting pants.
[22]A cap of Turkish origin worn by many Muslims.
[23]Worthy.

Commentary

The last possibility a person considers is that he could be wrong. It is a common tendency to alight upon the first solution to a problem that appears right. Questioning the obvious is an essential tool in avoiding this pitfall.

Tabiyat de Rangeen (Fond of Variety)

Banta Singh went to purchase the national flag for putting up outside his house on Independence Day. The shopkeeper showed him flags of various sizes.

After examining them all, Banta remarked, '*Kaka, ae de vich do char hor vi* color *nahin haige tere kole? Yaar dukan'ch z'ra v'raity ta rakkhya kar* (don't you have some choice of colors in this? You should at least keep some variety).'

Commentary

Fascination with variety is relatively new in human history. For most of humanity's existence, it was 'Form follows Function', as the famous saying goes. That this was the dominant idea even well into the industrial age is made clear by Henry Ford's famous quote to customers buying his car, 'You can have any color so long it's black.'

Variety is essential in some things, but an endless quest for variety is as stultifying as its lack. A superficial variety may hide a more significant monolith underneath.

As someone remarked about America, it has thirty-one flavors of ice-cream, but just two political parties!

The Reluctant Olympian

Just as the Punjab Mail was pulling out of New Delhi railway station one evening, the passengers saw three sardars running down the track at full tilt, chasing the train. Though burdened with some light luggage, they were yet making a determined sprint, which was a pleasure to watch. The passengers cheered them on and rooted for them as they ran after the train.

At long last, one of them made a hell-for-leather dash, and in a desperate final burst of speed managed to throw his bag on to the doorway of the last compartment of the train and clamber on to it himself. A remarkable feat by any reckoning. The passengers caught him by his arms and pulled him in as they cheered. By this time the train had picked up speed and the other two could no longer hope to catch it. This youngster waved to them and collapsed on a seat to catch his breath.

The whole cabin had broken out in spontaneous applause at his effort, with many remarking this was exactly the kind of never-say-die spirit that was sorely missing in our sports teams.

'You should be in the Olympics instead of some of the *nikamme*[24] they send,' someone said. Others agreed, vigorously.

---

[24]Nincompoops.

But it took ten more minutes of gasping before the young man could recover his breath. His first words were, 'Oye ^&%$^!!!' Followed by '*^%^&&.' Then, after a pause, '*^^&&&.'

The fellow passengers were surprised at this *gaal*-fest. Instead of acknowledging their congratulations and praise, this young man was hurling some serious Punjabi abuse.

Finally he was fit enough to speak.

'*Jaana ta onnannu si. Assan sirf chharhaan vaaste aayen san* (they were the ones who were supposed to go. I only came to see them off)!'

Commentary

Similar to our Milkha Singh and the thief story, this illustrates the lurking monomania inherent in all our thinking. Sometimes one item on the agenda takes up all our attention and effort; sometimes one question on the question paper eats up all our time; sometimes one person in our life exhausts our entire emotional space.

Intelligence dictates that we periodically examine and rebalance our time, effort, expenditure, and other allocations. Experience tells us we don't.

This joke also illustrates how we might be chasing old demons that have long ceased to be relevant. For example, as soon as he saw his friends had missed the train, this young man ought to have stopped running. But being totally focused on his own sprint, he failed to see they had given up, and that the whole purpose had been defeated.

A 'Figger' of Speech

At the International Science Conference, various countries were presenting their progress.

'We have invented an aircraft that can touch the sky,' began the American, to huge applause.

'Sky? Really?' asked Dr Banta Singh, who was attending the conference for the first time.

The American smiled. 'Just a figure of speech, Dr Singh,' he said. 'I meant it can fly close to the stratosphere, give or take a few hundred feet ...'

The audience applauded again.

Next came the Russian. 'In my country we've invented a vessel that can travel along the ocean floor,' he said.

'The bottom of the ocean? Really?' asked Banta.

'Oh, nyet, nyet. Don't take everything so literally. Just a figure of speech. Give or take a few hundred feet, I mean,' said he.

After many similar claims, it was finally India's turn. Banta Singh went up to the rostrum and declared, 'In India we have always eaten through our noses.'

Pandemonium in the hall.

'Oye, calm down, calm down. Just a *figger* of speech,' he said soothingly. 'Say a couple of inches below ...'

Commentary

A perfect example of Karl Marx's notion of a quantitative change resulting in qualitative change. Here Banta Singh cleverly debunks the sensational exaggeration of his American and Russian counterparts. While doing so he also skirts the basics of calculus, illustrating the difference between continuous and discontinuous functions.

The Postman Spirit

Banta Singh has built a nice house after his retirement, but far away from the town, up in the hills. So far away, in fact, that the postman comes only if there is any mail to be brought; it is a ten-kilometer bicycle ride each way.

One day a friend sends a big and heavy parcel for Banta's birthday, and the poor postman has no choice but to pedal all the way up in the hot sun to Banta's house carrying it.

Banta thanks the postman for the parcel, gives him *baksheesh*[25], offers him a cold lassi and asks him to rest a few minutes before heading back. He then apologizes for making him do this long trip in the sun.

He also has a suggestion, *'Daakiya ji, tuonnu aenni door aappe aan di ki lorh si? 'raam naal* post *ton pehj denna si ...* (Mr Postman, you shouldn't really have bothered coming all the way. You should have taken it easy and simply mailed it)!'

Commentary

As HL Mencken wrote, 'There is always a well-known solution to every human problem – neat, plausible, and wrong.'

---

[25]Tip.

What You See is What You Get (WYSIWYG)

Sardarji and sardarni sahiba are traveling by the train. It is morning, and sardarji excuses himself to use the bathroom. When he goes there the bathroom is actually vacant. He opens the door, sees the bathroom is occupied, apologizes, and returns. 'There's a sardar in there,' he tells his wife when he comes back. 'I'll try again in a few minutes.'

Every time he goes he finds the same sardar already in there. After half-an-hour and some ten attempts, his wife can't understand how this is happening; how could the bathroom remain occupied for so long?

She decides to check it out herself.

She goes to the bathroom, and returns in a fit of rage. She gives the sardarji a tight slap and commences a tirade in choice Punjabi, 'I know why you've been going there every two minutes. I've seen it all with my own eyes now. You've got a woman in there! Don't you dare deny it ...'

Commentary

Sometimes, no matter what the reality, all one sees is what one wants to see, which, literally in this case, is one's own reflection.

The joke further illustrates the fact that the same misunderstanding, however absurd, might afflict multiple people.

An Orderly Solution

Someone asks the sardarji the age-old question, *'Mai kya paji,* which came first, the chicken or the egg?'

Comes the reply, *'Oye ae vi koi s'vaal e* ^&%$^? *Je pehle* order *kitta ohi pehle auna* (what a stupid question. Whatever you order first will come first)!'

Commentary

Truly an Alexandrian solution. By taking the problem out of its traditional ivory tower construct and bringing it to the practical plane, the sardar gave a perfectly reasonable answer to a conundrum considered the ultimate in the realm of unanswerable questions.

Finishing the Job

Passengers on the Delhi-Amritsar Express were about to sit down to breakfast when suddenly they found their train leaving the railway track and going all across the countryside. Terrified as the train lurched this way and that, they held on to their seats and prayed for dear life. After about ten minutes of this, the train was suddenly back on track, and fortunately made it to Amritsar without any mishap, and only slightly behind schedule.

Upon reaching Amritsar a number of passengers complained to the authorities, who called in the driver to ask what had happened.

As you might expect, the driver was none other than Sardar Banta Singh.

A senior railway official asked him to explain these strange happenings. Banta Singh began, 'Sirjee, we were perfectly on time until I suddenly saw that a dog was sitting on the track about hundred feet ahead ...'

'You silly fellow,' the official scolded. 'You should have just run it over. You can't very well endanger the lives of hundreds of passengers to avoid some stray dog ...'

Banta Singh nodded vigorously in assent. '*Ahoji, ahoji. Aehoi mai vi sochaya si* (yes sir, yes sir. This is precisely what I thought too). But what could I do, sirjee, as the train approached, the dog got up from the tracks and began to run away into the fields ...'

Commentary

Einstein said that the invention of the atomic bomb had changed everything except our thinking.

When the cold war ended, America continued to pile up nuclear weapons as though the arms race was still on, refusing to rebalance its spending accordingly, redirecting its military budget toward civilian uplift to reflect the new context. It quickly became the largest debtor nation.

A chase or a race engages our attention so much that we forget its purpose. As with our engine driver here, we sometimes don't remember to shift gears to accommodate changed realities.

The Differential Gear

Banta Singh and his friends were discussing their travel plans. They were driving to Agra in Banta's fancy new car to see the Taj.

When asked how long the journey would take, Banta Singh told his friends he had budgeted four hours for the drive from Delhi to Agra, and some twenty hours for the return journey. The friends couldn't understand this. Why this difference, they asked. Would there be more traffic? Were they going to take another route back?

Banta Singh shook his head. None of these reasons, he said. '*Oye z'ra sochcho. Gaddi de agge de* gear *kinne hegen? Panj. Hor pichche de? Sirf ik. Hun hisaab laalo* (think a bit – how many forward gears does the car have? Five. And how many reverse gears? One. Now go figure).'

Commentary

Speaking of the travails of aging, Mark Twain is quoted as saying, 'It isn't so much that I forget things that happened. It is that I remember things that didn't.' Making a correlation where none exists is at least as perilous as missing ones that do. Five gears forward, one gear back. Agra – forward, Delhi – back. The mind is very good at subconscious associations.

Prepared for Anysingh

Sardarji had invited a dear old friend of his for breakfast one Sunday. The friend thought it was an informal affair and showed up dressed casually. When the servant opened the door, he could see the sardarji seated at the dining table, dressed formally in a coat and tie. He wondered if he had missed something and shown up for a formal occasion in the wrong clothes.

'You are all dressed up,' remarked the friend.

'Yes, yes,' replied the sardar. 'You know how it is ... I hold a high position. *Kadi kadi achaan'k koi khas vis'tor aa jaanda e* (and sometimes important visitors show up without an appointment).'

Then the phone rang and the sardarji rose to get it. The friend was surprised to see that he was wearing nothing but a *kachcha* (pair of shorts) under the coat!

The friend couldn't help asking about this discrepancy.

'*Kadi kadi koi ni vi aanda e* (sometimes no one shows up too),' explained the sardar.

Commentary

One of the biggest problems in thinking is what is called, 'atomicity',[26] what is considered indivisible. For example, there is no such thing as 'half a transaction', or crossing half the river. Naturally, what is 'atomic' changes over time, with the availability of new technologies, or even

---

[26]A throwback, perhaps, to a time when the atom was considered indivisible.

what becomes acceptable. Many new breakthroughs comprise entirely of taking something that was previously considered a composite and providing ways to use and access its component parts.

Who knows but that the sardar here was on the cusp of a new fashion trend in power dressing? After all, the tie, which used to be an essential element of formal attire in America and Europe has over the last few years become optional!

All for the Lord

This is from an old column by Khushwant Singh.

A Hindu, Muslim and Sikh priest were talking one day. The conversation came around to what they did with the money devotees put in the donation box.

'Ours is all fixed,' said the Muslim priest. 'I get to keep 5 percent of the proceeds. The rest goes to the mosque.'

'Ours is a little more chaotic,' smiled the Hindu priest. 'I take out all the money, put it in a pot, draw a circle on the ground, stand in the middle of the circle, and then throw the pot high in the air. Whatever falls outside the circle I get to keep, and whatever falls inside the circle belongs to the temple.'

Then came the bhaiji's turn.

'*Assi Ishwar naal aestraan dalali ni karde* (I do not do this commission business with God),' he declared grandly. 'I give everything over to Him.'

'Really!' the other two exclaimed. Then how do you manage ...'

The bhaiji continued. 'I take all the money from the collection, put it in a cloth bag, tie it up. Then I close my eyes and throw the bag up in the sky to God, saying, "O Waheguru,[27] everything is all yours. Keep whatever you want and send down to me only what you don't need."'

Commentary

The bhaiji has used a fantastic logical device made famous by Sherlock Holmes, 'When you eliminate the impossible, whatever remains, however improbable, is the truth.' Here, the tacit 'truth' agreed upon by all three divines is that God is in the sky (the term *ooper-wala*[28] is common throughout North India for God). Nor can the other two deny another 'truth', that God is infallible when he showers coins back on the bhaiji ...

Economisingh

Banta Singh was waiting at the bus stop returning from work. His house was about three kilometers away, and the bus rarely kept to schedule. He was delighted, therefore, when his bus showed up so soon after he had reached the bus stop.

---

[27] Almighty.

[28] Literally, 'the one above'.

Unfortunately, instead of coming to a stop, the bus slowed down just enough to let some passengers off, and then, even as he ran after it, kept moving. Banta Singh was determined to catch it at the next bus stop, which was only a couple of hundred yards away. He almost made it, but missed the bus once again by just a few yards. On a whim, he kept running after it, but the same thing kept happening at each bus stop.

Finally at one bus stop he caught up to the bus, but just as he made it to the doorway, he realized it was the stop where he was supposed to get off!

As he walked home sweating and panting from the bus stop, he had a realization. Not only had he gotten some much-needed exercise, he had saved ten rupees of bus fare! This was a pleasing thought, and he told his wife when he got home how he had run behind the bus instead of riding it, and thereby gotten his exercise for the day and also saved ten rupees in the bargain.

To his surprise, his wife was not pleased. Instead of praising him, she got upset.

'Hai rabba (oh, God), you are so foolish,' she sighed. 'Couldn't you have run after a taxi? Imagine! You could have saved us two hundred rupees instead of ten!'

Commentary

A monumental joke.

To me, this ranks right up there in consequence with the first joke in this collection. It takes aim at the entire notion of notional measurement, which encompasses so much of modern cultural and economic discourse – relative stock market and other valuations, and even things like the Consumer Confidence Index, all often no more than interconnected 'feelings'.

Years ago *Time Magazine* carried a piece[29] on the mythology of winning and losing in our day. In the mid-1980s New York real estate-mogul Mortimer Zuckerman won a hard-fought battle to secure a huge project. He was declared a winner. Then, owing to some bureaucratic wrangling, his project was delayed. They declared him a loser. Shortly thereafter the real estate market tanked. Unlike many other builders, Zuckerman emerged unscathed precisely because he had not executed the project. So he had gone from 'winner' to 'loser' to 'winner' in the space of a few months, all without moving from where he was!

'Are you better off than you were four years ago?' the candidate asks the audience. It is a question to which there is no precisely measurable answer, only a notion. Depending on which set of facts one includes, one might receive diametrically opposite responses.

In Plane Sight

A pilot and his deputy are landing a plane at night at an unfamiliar airport in Africa. As they approach, the senior pilot Capt Banta Singh surveys the airport and remarks urgently to the junior Bachittar Singh, 'Oye, Bachittara, you had better let *me* do this. This runway is extremely short. These Africans don't build anything right.'

---

[29]'Spectator the Agony of Victory' by Kurt Andersen, *Time*, 17 Jan 1994.

After some intense maneuvering and many anxious moments, Banta manages to land the plane safely. As he taxies to the terminal, he turns to his copilot and says, '*Hore vekh, khotteyan ne* runway *banatti sirf* 100 *gaj lambi, te chauri* ^&%$^ *1000 gaj* (and look, the fools have made the runway just a hundred yards long, but it is ^&%$^ thousand yards wide)!'

Commentary

The joke illustrates three common tendencies – (a) to lock ourselves into a solution (b) to look for the fault everywhere but at home, and (c) presume a design is good or bad because of where it belongs.

Long ago, I remember an Indian roommate of mine at an American university telling another Indian friend, if you find yourself forcing a carton or bottle cap open, stop and think if you are doing it wrong, because Americans usually design things to be easy to use. It was good advice.

Here, Banta and Bachittar did not think to provide the same courtesy to Africans.

The Funeral Procession

The foreigner thought this was the strangest funeral procession he had ever seen. Instead of sad and serious faces, he saw smiles and laughs. Instead of people walking slowly behind the cortege, he saw dancing, music, fists in the air. He was puzzled.

Summoning up the courage to stop one of the mourners, he asked, 'Excuse me. I've never seen a funeral procession with so many happy people. Is that the tradition in your country?'

'No, you are right,' said the sardar. 'Our funerals too are usually sad and serious affairs. But this is a special occasion. It is the first time that a sardar has died of brain tumor.'

Commentary

Ridiculous, isn't it?

Then consider this: A developing country like India, where around 50 percent of the population does not have clean drinking water and 60 per cent has no access to a decent toilet, spends a reported 30,000 crores (roughly $7 billion) on the 2010 Commonwealth Games extravaganza, building state-of-the-art stadiums and airports, because it thinks these would prove to the world that it is an emerging superpower!

Power-cut Ordeals

The discussion at the bar veered round to the worst personal experiences with power failures. The Frenchman spoke about how he had once got caught in the Paris underground railway during a blackout.

The American told them how he had to spend three hours trapped in an elevator inside of a New York skyscraper when the lift had stopped working.

'That's nothing,' answered Banta Singh, flooring them both with an account of how he had once been stranded on an escalator for five hours, when the power had failed at a Chandigarh[30] mall.

Commentary

As the saying goes, 'Better to keep quiet and let people wonder if one is a fool than open one's mouth and remove all doubt.'

Not Cool

A newly-married sardar wants to take his bride out to a classy restaurant. As he is just starting out in life, however, he does not have too much money to splurge. So he tells her they'll stop there for just a cup of coffee.

'Two coffees, piping hot,' he orders for both when they are seated at the unfamiliarly plush seats. The waiter returns with the order, and they start sipping their cups. The coffee is really, really hot. As he waits for the coffee to cool, the sardar, out of idle curiosity, takes a casual glance at the menu. Suddenly, he becomes all agitated and tells his wife, 'Drink quickly, drink quickly. We've to drink it up before it gets cold.'

She doesn't understand why. When she tries to ask, he merely says 'drink quickly' again, urgently. They finish somehow,

---

[30]Capital of Punjab and Haryana.

with their mouths all burnt. The sardar gestures for the bill, hastily pays it, and hurries out with his wife.

She has tears in her eyes from the scalding, and wants to know as soon as they get out what that was all about.

'It says the hot coffee costs ten rupees but the cold coffee is fifty rupees,' he explains. 'Am I stupid to shell out an extra eighty rupees for nothing?'

Commentary

Paranoia is a potent force, which can tie us into all kinds of situations that a moment of calm reflection would dispel. This is accentuated by unfamiliar circumstances, and given a further boost by inherent suspicion that is part of the human makeup.

Cost of Luggage

The sardar reached the bus stop and wanted to catch a taxi to his destination. The taxi driver quoted a price of two hundred rupees, plus twenty rupees for the luggage.

Sardarji put his luggage on the taxi, and said, 'Oye, here is the address, here's twenty rupees for the luggage. Just deliver it there. I'll take the bus.'

Commentary

Though it doesn't work in this particular example, the idea of breaking out portions of a service or product that initially is one integrated whole is hardly new. Even here, is it not conceivable that the taxi could be used as a luggage transporter, perhaps shared by multiple passengers? Here the sardar is just exploring some 'outside the box' options, pardon the pun.

Stamp Duty

Some decades ago, the Indian Post and Telegraph Department introduced an overnight service to major cities, called 'Quick Mail Service'. Special mailboxes were set up for the purpose, and for a slightly higher cost a letter would be delivered the next day to any major Indian city. When he heard of it Banta Singh had a sudden brainwave. A quick calculation told him that the postage to send the equivalent of his weight via QMS from Delhi to Bombay was cheaper than the cost of a train ticket.

He went to the post office and purchased enough stamps to mail his own weight. After sticking them all on his forehead, he went to the closest QMS mailbox and attempted to mail himself. This is how the mailman found him when he came to collect the mail, head pushed into the mouth of the mailbox.

'Hey, you, out-of-the-way, I need to get at the mailbox,' the postman said.

Banta's head was stuck, and he was trying to get into the postbox, not out. After many polite attempts to persuade him to step aside, the mailman, patience exhausted, felt

other measures were called for, and gave him a kick on the bottom. Just about this time, Banta's head sprang loose from the mailbox.

'What kind of *nikamma* (incompetent) postman are you?' he said angrily when he eyed the postman. '*Tik't mathe de utte lagya e, tuon mor ^&%$^ putthe pa riya e* (the stamps are on my forehead, and here you are canceling my bottom instead)!'

Commentary

Bernard Shaw said, 'The reasonable man adapts himself to the world; the unreasonable one persists in trying to adapt the world to himself. Therefore, all progress depends on the unreasonable man.' The sardar here was merely anticipating the idea of the courier service by a few years.

The Regimental Guard

'Every one of my brothers is in the regiment, sir,' says Karpal Singh, the new recruit, proudly, as he reports to his English officer upon joining the regiment.

'Sepoy Corp'l Singh, *tumhara bhai log sab ka naam kya haai* (Corp'l Singh, what are the names of all your brothers)?' asks Capt Paul Wilson in clipped Hindustani, being himself the scion of a three-generation Punjab Regiment household.

'Sir, eldest is Jarnail Singh, then Karnail Singh, after that Major Singh, then Kaptan Singh then Laptan Singh, sir.'

'Wah, wah, wah. God bless your dear mother. Quite the Regimental Supply Corps, isn't she?'

'Sir, no, sir. She is Kulwant Kaur.'

Commentary

Sepoy Karpal Singh is either being pleasantly naive, or else exhibiting a level of suavity that would do credit to a career diplomat. Kulwant means 'benefactor of the race'.

A Private Joke

Passengers on the Frontier Mail were woken up at 6 a.m. to a torrent of abuse. An angry sardar was screaming at the train conductor, who was listening calmly, only smiling silently from time to time, but offering neither an explanation nor shouting back.

After a little while, some passengers tried to restrain the angry man. 'Look at what he has done,' the sardar shouted to them. 'He was supposed to wake me up before Ambala two hours ago. I had to get down there. *Ooparon hasda e* ^&%$^ (on top of it you laugh) ...' he started off again.

The train conductor remained silent, smiling and shaking his head. This was too much even for the other passengers. 'Okay, TC sahib, so you made a mistake. That doesn't mean you have to take all this abuse,' they said. Finally, he broke his silence.

'This is nothing, sirjee,' he said. 'I'm just thinking about the passenger on the next berth whom I did wake up at Ambala and hustled off the train along with his luggage. This is nothing compared to the *gaali* that sardarji must be giving me!'

Commentary

Sardar Parkash Singh Badal was the Union agriculture minister in the cabinet of Prime Minister Morarji Desai. In a few months, state assembly elections were held in Punjab, and Badal quit the Union cabinet to become the chief minister of the state. He was replaced as Union agriculture minister by Sardar Surjeet Singh Barnala. Next day well-known newspaper cartoonist RK Laxman had the prime minister addressing a group of sardars, 'One of you is the union agriculture minister!'

The point being, it was somehow stuck in everybody's head that the agriculture minister had to be a Sikh. Such stereotyping is not unfamiliar, and often done without malice. In this instance, the train conductor had made a mental note to wake the sardarji up and make sure he got down at his early-morning stop.

Only, early in the morning, he had picked the wrong sardar to render this service.

Detachment

There has been some communal frenzy in the neighborhood, but sardarji is just returning from work from out-of-town, and knows nothing yet of the mayhem that has been afoot all day in his locality.

As he gets down at his bus stop, one of his neighbors spots him, and informs him, 'Sardarji, there is terrible *danga-fasad*[31] going on here. They have set fire to Bachittar Singh's house next door to you!'

Sardarji replies calmly, *'Ta mainnu ki* (so what's it to me)?'

The neighbor staggers away, stunned by this indifference.

Minutes later the same neighbor comes back running, with even more panic written all over his face.

'Sardar sahib, now they are setting fire to your house!' he screams, trembling with urgency.

'Ta tainnu ki (so what is it to you)?' comes the reply.

Commentary

This illustrates how there can be an element of mental detachment[32] even in the midst of seeming selfishness. The fact that the sardar

---

[31]Fighting, turmoil.

[32]The joke echoes the story attributed in the Mahabharata to King Janaka, one of legendary mental equipoise. Told that his capital is ablaze, Janaka replies, *'Mithilaayaam pradeeptaayaam na mae dahyati kinchana'* which, when you get right down to it, is just *Ta mainnu ki* in fancy Sanskrit.

is as calm about his own tragedy as he seems to be about the one befalling his neighbor underscores the inescapable fact that ultimately, each of us has to face our own problems.

Wise Counsel

Constable Banta Singh is asked to rush to the scene of an accident and take charge. It is a terrible affair. Two people are dead, and several seriously injured. He finds a man crying in pain because his leg is broken. Banta tries to pacify him by offering some perspective. 'Oye z'ra sabar karo, sabar karo (calm down, calm down). You have just hurt a leg and for that you are making such a huge fuss ... Woh do bandeyaan nu vekho (look at those two people),' he says, pointing to the two bodies. 'They have lost their lives, but do you see them making any noise over it?'

Commentary

To gain perspective, by one definition, is to step far enough away. Some perspectives are from an absurdly long distance; to anyone's thinking there is hardly anything farther away than death. But the absurd can often shed significant light on our thinking, as evident in geometry, where the principle of reductio ad absurdum is applied frequently. In short, Banta is pointing out to the injured man that he could well have been one of those two bodies, and thus asking him to count his blessings.

Beating the Second Law[33]

'How do you keep a sardar occupied?' asked someone.

'Give him a piece of paper with "PTO"[34] written on both sides,' came the answer.

Commentary

How often we are caught up in our immediate circumstances, forgetting to step back and look at the larger picture! For several decades now the people of Tamilnadu (India), for example, have been bouncing back and forth between two ruling political parties, both renowned for corruption and malfeasance. When they tire of one party they forget how angry they were with the other party till just a while ago, and vote it back into office in a landslide. Similar is the case of the USA with Democrats and Republicans, or in Britain between Labour and Conservatives.

A lack of memory and imagination, and the mantra of lesser evil, are at the heart of this, more so at a time when the attention spans are increasingly getting shorter.

---

[33]Of Thermodynamics, which says that perpetual motion is impossible in an independent system.

[34]PTO (*Please Turn Over*) is the standard acronym in India to indicate to the reader that there is more on the other side of the page. It is the same as *Overleaf* ... in America.

Identity Crisis – III

During the Punjab turmoil of the '90s, there was a particularly bold and gruesome daylight killing of a top police official by the Khalistanis.[35] The president of India, Giani Zail Singh, was beside himself with grief, having known the official personally during his time as Punjab chief minister. He was anxious that the murderers be caught and punished. To convey his sense of urgency, that very afternoon a telegram was sent to the Punjab government directly from Rashtrapati Bhavan,[36] 'GIANIJI ORDERS STOP APPREHEND ALL CULPRITS IMMEDIATELY AT ANY COST STOP TREAT TOP PRIORITY STOP.'

The telegraph dispatcher at Delhi was a sardar who was somewhat proud of his English. He decided to proofread the statement handed to him and make some spelling corrections.

In the next twenty-four hours, every unfortunate soul by the name of Kulpreet Singh anywhere within Punjab found himself in custody.

Commentary

'Be careful about reading health books. You can die of a misprint' – Mark Twain

---

[35]Those fighting for Khalistan, a separate Sikh homeland.
[36]The Indian presidential palace.

Milk-a Singh

The annual Punjab Agricultural Fair featured a prize cow competition, with medals for the finest bovine specimens.

Someone claimed that his cow gave twenty-four liters, another that his cow gave twenty liters, someone else nineteen liters, and so on.

Banta Singh also entered his cow, which he claimed gave two liters.

When asked how he hoped to win with such a low number, he countered, *'Oye madj di k'raecter vi koi cheez hondi e ke ni* (doesn't the animal's character count for something)?'

Commentary

To Banta, in this example, the 'character' of the cow was paramount. It demonstrates a sentience growing rarer by the day in an industry where animals (and people) are viewed as mere producing cogs, where animals are kept in the cruelest conditions in the pursuit of what is called, 'factory farming'.

On a larger canvas, it demonstrates the importance of asking the question, 'By what measure?'

Practically every part of the world is chasing after a notional commodity called the GDP. The small kingdom of Bhutan on the other hand, has introduced a new measure called GNH, or, Gross National Happiness. Clearly, the measures, and the winners emerging thereby, will be quite different.

Compromisingh

A large contingent of sardars from Gwalior was heading on a holiday to Amritsar. Owing to some poor planning, all of them reached Gwalior railway station just a few minutes before the train was to leave. In a rush, the entire lot of them crowded into the last compartment.

On its way north, the train had to pass over an ancient bridge already weakened by the torrential monsoon that year. An overcrowded compartment was literally the last straw. The bridge collapsed as the train was passing over it, the last compartment fell in, and there were a large number of casualties.

It was one of the worst accidents ever for the Indian railways. Naturally, there was a huge outcry over such a preventable tragedy.

There was a furore in the Indian Parliament, as questions were raised about how this could all have happened. Eventually, a group of MPs,[37] all sardars, put their heads together and came up with a draft resolution which they thought would prevent such problems in the future.

It read, 'Hereafter there shall be no last compartment on the Indian Railways.'

The Indian Parliament debated this motion for many days; impassioned speeches were made for and against. Finally a

---

[37]Members of Parliament.

senior minister, the evergreen Sardar Swaran Singh,[38] proposed a compromise resolution seeking to satisfy all sides.

'I have close knowledge of the Indian Railways,' he began as he rose to speak. 'I know this is not an easy thing to do. But I also understand the strong sentiments of members in the wake of the tragedy. I would therefore humbly suggest the following amendment:

'We shall urge the railways to set up a panel to recommend how best to eliminate the last compartment from their trains. And if after studying the issue they still find this impossible to do, they should endeavor to move the last compartment to somewhere in the middle.'

Commentary

The joke illustrates the distinction between the desirable and the doable. Some things cannot be legislated, as King Canute[39] demonstrated to his courtiers. It also shows the fallacy of thinking that mishaps can be eliminated with a wave of a wand; by abolishing this or ordaining that, whereas the surest safeguard against them is a culture of alertness, rule-following, and maintenance.

But a literal reading of Sardar Swaran Singh's words is not without an underlying lesson. Some existing solutions are best re-thought, not just tinkered with. What these are is a choice that should be made

---

[38]One of the longest serving members of the Indian cabinet, from 1952–1975. He held many portfolios, including Defense, Food, External Affairs and Railways. He was renowned as a calm and able negotiator.

[39]King Canute of England, who is said to have taught his flatterers a lesson when they kept proclaiming his omnipotence. He sat on the seashore and ordered the tide to roll back.

wisely, and sparingly. In many modern cities people spend considerable amounts of time commuting to and from work. The standard solution appears to be to add more lanes, a fix that always turns out to be temporary as traffic grows even heavier. The obvious solution of people working close to where they live seems to elude city planning experts everywhere, perhaps because it seems too ridiculously simple.

Milk-a Singh – II

Another competition at the same fair was about how well someone could milk a cow. The contestants were each given a large container, and lots were drawn at random to assign each to a different cowshed. At the end of half-an-hour, it would be measured how much milk each had gathered.

At the end of the allotted time the various competitors returned with their milk containers. The results ranged from twenty-five liters to seventeen liters; it was found that all had gathered respectable amounts of milk except Banta Singh, whose container barely held anything.

Interviewed afterwards, he fumed to reporters, 'Oye ^&%$^, *mainnu saand kinne fadatta* (dammit, who stuck me with a bull)!'

Commentary

The first rule of troubleshooting is: If you run into a problem that you realize you cannot fix, it is wisest to appeal for help sooner rather than later.

Believability Olympics

Since there is an Olympics for everything else these days, someone thought to organize a competition for telling the most unbelievable story. Many stalwarts participated, including some famous news anchors. Each contestant got to speak for two minutes, and in the end the judges would award the gold medal for the most unbelievable story.

'I jumped over the moon,' began one contestant, continuing with what he saw on the other side, how he came across aliens, and so on. They stopped him after two minutes.

'I fought hand to hand with Alexander the Great,' began another, and kept the audience engrossed as each incident he related seemed more fantastic than the last. 'Two minutes,' called the judge. The contender sat down to applause.

And so on it continued. Then one young fellow stood up to tell his tall tale.

'Once I saw two sardars playing chess,' he started.

The judges briefly looked at each other and nodded. Then the chief judge stood up and said, 'This competition is over. Congratulations to you, young man' as he handed him the gold medal.

Commentary

The unbelievable does not have to be exotic; it could just be something unthought of earlier.

Aise Math Karo

It is the annual conference of sardars, with the world's media in full attendance.

The emcee, a sardar, is in full pride mode. 'People think that sardars have an aversion to mathematics,' he says. 'I am here to show you this is far from true. Sardars can do mathematics as well as anyone else.'

He continues, 'To demonstrate this, I'm going to ask for a volunteer to come up to the stage.' Several hands go up, and he chooses one gentleman, who comes up to the dais and is seated near a microphone.

After asking his name (Banta Singh) and where he lives (Delhi), the emcee says, 'I'm going to ask you a few simple mathematics questions so the world can see any average sardar is reasonably proficient in math. Shall we start?'

Banta nods his head. 'First question, what is 100 times 100?'

Pat comes the answer: '78.'

The emcee is obviously disappointed, but he is a seasoned campaigner and knows how to paper over glitches of this kind. 'You are nervous, as anyone would be. Take a deep breath and relax. Let's give this young man another chance, shall we, ladies and gentleman,' he says. The audience roars its approval.

'Let's try again. What is 10 times 10?' he asks.

This time Banta thinks for a whole minute. Finally he answers, '95?'

'You're getting really close,' says the emcee, trying his best. Let's give him one more chance, shall we?'

The audience roars, 'Yes! Yes! Yes! Give him another chance!'

'OK. Final chance, Bantaji. What is 5 times 5?'

Now Banta thinks for a whole three minutes. Suspense grows. A pin-drop silence in the huge convention *shamiana*.[40] Then he says tentatively, '25?'

Before the emcee can say anything, his voice is drowned by the roar of the audience, 'Give him another chance! Give him another chance! Give him another chance!'

Commentary

The joke illustrates the folly of doing something to impress someone else. To the contrary, such contrived displays only serve to draw attention to our own discomfort with who we are, and to the perceived shortcomings that cause us such anguish.

Elevating Form over Function fails every time.

Foreign Exchange

'I had a terrible night on the train,' said Banta Singh to his friend who had come to receive him at the station. 'I had an upper berth, and you know how I get dizzy up there.'

'That's terrible. You should have exchanged places with the person on the lower berth ...' said Santa.

---

[40]Tent.

'*Aehoi soche mai saari raat intezaar kar riya si. Magar axchange karan vaste koi banda* ^&%$^ *labh'ya hi nahi, thalle da* seat *peya khaali khaali* (oh, I sat up all night waiting for someone, but there was no one to exchange with, the lower berth was empty),' replied Banta.

Commentary

Sometimes we are so geared up to tackle a problem that we are unable to cope with its non-existence. You arrive all prepared or to argue vehemently with somebody, only to discover that the other person agrees with you! Now you don't know what to say, because your carefully prepared speech has been suddenly made irrelevant. It happens more often than we think that we are responding from some preconceived expectations, rather than to the situation on the ground (or in this case, on the train).

The Japanese martial art of Judo is based exactly on this principle.

Ab Woh Z'mana G'ya

Every day around lunchtime, Banta Singh would buy a *katori* (bowl) of *dahi* (curd) from the shop to take and eat in the park.

Every day on his way to the park some pranksters at a tea stall along the way would ask him for the time.

Banta Singh would turn his left wrist to look at his watch. '*Pahran baje* (twelve noon),' he would announce. Meanwhile, the *dahi* he was carrying in his left hand would overturn and spill.

After a few days he mentioned this to his wife. She slapped her forehead in frustration and said, 'You could have refused to tell the time. Or if you had to show off your watch, couldn't you at least transfer the *dahi* to your right hand first?' Banta Singh couldn't wait to try out this strategy.

The next day someone asked him for the time again, as he was heading to the park with the *dahi*. First Banta Singh transferred the *dahi* to the right hand. Then he dismissed the stranger with a contemptuous flick of his right hand, saying, '*Bewakoof banane da ou zamana ta g'ya. Hun time-wime ni halle kiseenu dasna* (the days are past when I could be fooled. No telling the time to anybody any more).'

Commentary

What is the difference between education and training? The former gives you the background and the tools to contend with unscripted situations. The latter, by definition, is intended to equip you to do a specific, known task. Both are needed to make our way in the world, but it is not always easy to tell when to use which. For example, it would usually be a waste for someone to spend a lot of time thinking about a job that has already been well-understood. On the other hand, it is important to guard against the tendency to assume any new situation to be just a mild variant of the old. A fluid transition between the two skills is probably the essence of intelligence. As for this joke, focusing on the details and forgetting about the larger purpose is the theme of the adage, 'missing the wood for the trees'.

What's in a Name?

Banta Singh had triplets, all three bonny boys. His wife asked what they should name them.

'Let's call the first one Harminder Singh, after my *chacha*,'[41] he said.

'Gurminder Singh for the second, after your grandfather,' he continued. She was very happy.

'And the third we have to call Mao-Tse Tung,' he said, with a resigned air.

His wife asked, 'What? Why some strange name?'

'*Oye biwi*, don't you know that every third child born in the world is Chinese?' said Banta.

Commentary

The trouble is, there are many truths in the world, and we are saddled with deciding whether, when, and which to apply in a particular situation.

A Matter of Principal

Sardarji won the state lottery. His ten-rupee ticket had won fifteen lakh[41] rupees. When he went to claim it the chap at

---

[41]A lakh is the Hindustani for 1,00,000 (one hundred thousand).

the lottery agency said he would get fourteen lakh rupees after deducting tax.

Sardarji became very puzzled by this twist at first, then angry. He said there was no mention of any deductions when the ticket was sold. As far as he was concerned he should get fifteen lakhs as advertised on the billboards.

The lottery agency tried to explain to him that this was the norm, and if he had asked the lottery-ticket vendor he would have explained it to him. The sardarji would have none of it. Many hours of argument ensued.

At the end of it, sardarji had had enough. '*Oye,* just give me back my ten rupees,' he declared, banging his fist on the desk.

Commentary

Pragmatism or principle? It is a more difficult dilemma than may seem when one is not faced with it.

The legend of Yudhisthira being prepared to forgo heaven itself rather than entering it without his loyal companion (a stray dog), is regarded in India as the ultimate example of upholding principle even at a supreme cost. It is equally wise to bear in mind the practical words of Thomas Jefferson, who cautioned that every difference of opinion is not a difference of principle.

Most people would say getting fourteen lakhs instead of fifteen upon an investment of ten rupees was still quite good. In this case the clerk said it was a tax withholding. It could just as easily have been a demand for a bribe to release the money. What should the sardarji have done then?

It is no exaggeration to say that the average answer to that question is as accurate a reflection of a society as any single measure can be.

What's in a Name? – II

Every morning a sardarji could be seen walking three Alsatians[42] around the Bombay stadium track. They were magnificent animals; beautiful to look at, and superbly well-trained besides.

After having admired the dogs from a distance for several days, a dog-lover finally decided to go up to the sardarji and talk to him about his pets. He first asked if the dogs would bite, and the sardarji assured him they would not unless commanded.

'What are they called?' he asked the sardar.

'Well, this is Raminder Singh, this is Harvinder Singh, and this is Baljinder Singh,' said the sardar, pointing to each Alsatian in turn.

The man was a little surprised, if touched, by the sardarji's evident love for his dogs. Clearly his affection for them extended to thinking of them as no mere animals. What an emancipated state of mind, the man said to himself.

His reverie was interrupted. '*Hore main ji Tauni* (and by the way, sir, I'm Tony),' said the sardarji, extending his hand as he introduced himself.

Commentary

The joke here has to do somewhat with the fact that most urban sardars (Punjabi boys, more generally) have a short informal name by which they are called at home – Billoo, Bittoo, Cuckoo, Babloo, Teetoo, Tony, being some of the more common ones.

---

[42]An old Indian name for German Shepherds.

On a broader scale it highlights the fact that we have multiple personas within the same individual, even if we are not schizophrenic.

Optimisingh

It was sardarji's first day on the job, and the boss was pleased to see the new hire still hard at work as he left at 6 p.m. He made a mental note to call in the young man the following day and praise him for his dedication.

The next morning the boss called the sardarji and said he was pleased to see him working so diligently. 'What were you working on?' he asked, casually, seeking to put the nervous new recruit at ease.

'Sirjee, I found the keys on all our computer keyboards were not arranged in alphabetical order. I was here till midnight, but I set every one of them right,' said the sardar proudly.

Commentary

High speed and efficiency are wonderful ... if one is heading in the right direction. As the saying goes, doing the right thing comes before doing things right. And while we're on the theme of adages, let's not forget the old reliable, measure twice, and cut once.

Banta Singh, Secret Agent

Once Banta Singh and his wife were sitting in a hotel room in a foreign country. The television was on, and they were watching the news.

Suddenly, Banta got up, and putting a finger to his lips to indicate that she should keep quiet, he proceeded to look all around the room, including under the bed, on the ceiling and the walls, the furniture and the gadgets.

Finally he beckoned to his wife to come out of the room and meet him in the corridor. When she came out, she wanted to know what was going on.

'The room is bugged,' he whispered.

'Why do you say that?,' whispered his wife. 'We are just here on vacation, nobody even knows about it.'

'The tv guys somehow seem to know everything we are doing. Didn't you hear when they said, *"You are watching CNN?"* '

Commentary

Only the Paranoid Survive, goes the title of a book by a high-tech titan. Perhaps there's something to it when it comes to high level business or politics. But the other half of the story is that paranoia makes for a very stressful survival. It also makes you view the world in an incredibly skewed fashion, leading to the kinds of distortion illustrated by this joke.

The Book Critic

Banta Singh borrowed a book from the library. He kept on renewing it, before finally returning it after six months. He dropped it with a gesture of disgust into the return box at the library, where it landed with a big 'thud'.

'How did you enjoy your novel?' asked the librarian who had heard the noise.

Banta gave a sad shake of the head. 'Totally useless. Complete waste of time. Too many *k'raecters* (characters), no story or plot. Terrible, just terrible,' he replied.

'Oh, that's too bad. What book was it anyway?' she asked sympathetically.

'Something called Delhi Telephone Directory,' he replied.

Commentary

Context is everything. Fashion trumps all. Let some fancy literary critic write in *The New Yorker* of the 'searing honesty and breathtaking originality' of the same Delhi Telephone Directory, and everybody would accord it the status of a cultural landmark. The amount of unreadable stuff (yes, including this) which passes for literature is beyond measure.

Not going Swimmingly

Banta Singh and Bachittar Singh were taking an evening walk when they saw a remarkable sight. One of their neighbors, a sardar, was rowing a boat strenuously. As he plied the oars his face would contort with the effort. A loud grunt accompanied each movement of the arm indicating a struggle against the current.

Except ... this was on dry land – in the middle of his front lawn. Passersby were stopping, enjoying the comedy and making snide remarks.

Banta was furious at the sight. He said to Bachittar, '*Oye Bachittara, aihoje bewakoof* sardar **&*^%* *saare sardaaraan da na'an badnaam karde ne* (**&^&%* hey Bachittar, he is precisely the kind of imbecile sardar who makes all sardars a laughing stock).'

Bachittar Singh was nodding in agreement, when Banta Singh added, '*Je mai tair sakda taan siddha jaake kas ke ik rapta paana si ais %$%^&* nu* (if only I knew how to swim, I'd go and give this &*&*^ guy a tight slap right now)!'

Commentary

Isn't it surprising how the nature of outrage to the same thing differs so widely? A late friend of mine, the scientist and philosopher to whom this book is dedicated, noted that we are likely to be irritated most by those shortcomings in others which we ourselves possess.

Index of Progress

In the early 1950s a sardarji returned from England after a short visit. Friends in Amritsar asked him what he thought of the place.

'*Vaddi* advance *mulk e ji*,' he said, with the classic expression of Punjabi certitude: right hand above the right ear, eyebrows raised, eyes shut, pouting lower lip and a sideways tilt of the head. '*Oththe nikka tuon nikka bachcha vi t'hait angrezi bolda e* (a very advanced country. Even the tiniest child there speaks fluent English).'

Commentary

This has to do with the association of English in the Indian mind with advancement, progress, erudition, and other positive features.

Not All-at-Sea

Sardarji was showing off his new farmhouse to guests who had come to his housewarming party.

As he brought them round to the backyard they were surprised to see not one but two large swimming pools. Even as they were wondering about this they noticed another peculiar feature: one pool was full of water, as you would expect. But the other was completely dry. They advanced various theories to each other about the need for the two pools, before finally asking their host why this was so.

'*Vekhoji* it is *simpal* (simple). This pool,' he said, pointing to the one without water, 'is for those who don't know how to swim.'

Commentary

Wet:Dry::Swimmer:Non-swimmer.

What a logical association! Life unfortunately does not always follow logic. Indeed, except for artificially contrived situations, it rarely does.

In High Places

Four workmen are sitting on the steel girders on the seventy-ninth floor of a skyscraper under construction in Dubai. They're getting ready to eat lunch together.

The German opens his lunchbox first. He makes a grimace of anger and says, 'What? Bratwurst again! If I get bratwurst one more time I'm going to jump off this building.' Then he proceeds reluctantly to eat his lunch.

The Italian is next to open his lunchbox. He swears, saying, 'Mama mia, linguini again!!! If I get this tomorrow I'm going to jump straight down. I can't take it anymore.'

Then Banta Singh opens his lunch box . '*Phir o-hoi ^&%$^ saag paneer te mooli paranthe* (ONCE again ^&%$^ spinach-cheese and radish-parantha)! I agree with you. If I get it again I'm also going to jump down.'

The fourth guy merely listens as he eats his sandwich.

The following day they are sitting down to lunch at the same place.

The German opens his lunch box, utters a disgusted cry, saying, 'It's the same!' and leaps before anyone can say anything.

The Italian peeks into his lunchbox, and uttering an Italian oath he goes on to say, 'Same, same, same,' and steps off to his death.

Banta Singh opens his lunchbox, and utters a string of *gaalis*. 'It is the same once more,' he says in disgust as he jumps down.

The fourth workman is too shocked to say anything. After an hour in petrified silence, he slowly makes his way down.

Next day there is a funeral. The wives of the three dead workmen are there. The fourth workman has told everyone of the horror of what he saw.

'If only Stefan had told me,' weeps the German's wife, 'I'd have cooked absolutely anything he wanted. Oh why, oh why …'

'Alphonso never said a word to me,' cries the Italian's wife. 'I'd have made a gourmet meal every single day for him.' She sobs into her handkerchief.

'*Gal kuch s'majh ni aandi*,' says Jeeto. '*Sardarji sadde lainch 'mesha khud* pack *karde sun* … (I don't understand it … sardarji always packed his own lunch …)'

Commentary

An unfortunate consequence of attempting to keep up with the Joneses. Or should one say, going down with them?

Fed Up of Life?

One day Bachittar Singh went to meet Banta Singh. He wasn't at home, nor at his workplace, not even at any of his usual haunts. He was concerned because Banta had gone home very upset the previous evening after some land dispute.

Bachittar searched for his friend everywhere before locating him, finally. To his surprise, he found Banta Singh lying on the railway tracks.

'*Oye Banteya, aa kee kar riya e oye* (hey Banta, what's this you are doing, dude)?'

'*Oye Bachittara*, I'm through,' declared Banta. 'This is it for me. I'm just waiting for the 2:31 Express. When it comes *sadda filam da* 'The End' *ho juga* (my film will have its 'The End').'

After recovering from the initial shock, Bachittar tried to talk him out of this extreme course, but Banta would not listen. The 2:31 Express is it, he told Bachittar.

Then Bachittar decided to distract him by talking about something else. He noticed a large basket next to Banta, and asked him about it.

'*Aa kee e* (what's this)?

'Just some paratha and *saag paneer*, some dal, some *alu gobi*, and *kheer*, and a couple of *laddus*,' replied Banta.

'*Kaade vaste* (for what)?' Bachittar asked, his eyebrows knitted in curiosity.

'That train is always late. *Mai aithe lethe-lethe puhk naal* ^&%$^ *mar jaavaan* (should I lie here ^&%$^ dying of hunger)?'

Commentary

Ridiculous as the story appears, to me it yet seems full of insight. The train is going to arrive at some point for everyone. Except, like the proverbial Indian Railways quip,[43] we don't quite know when. Meanwhile we are busily engaged, full of self-importance in a flurry of activity, though dimly aware somewhere within of what awaits.

The joke punctures the entire pretense that is life – and death.

No Better

'*Kee kariye, biwi, saddi ta kismat hi khoti e* (what to do, wife, my luck is horrid only),' Banta Singh laments to his wife one morning at breakfast.

'What happened?' his wife wants to know.

'I lost one thousand rupees betting on the cricket match last night,' says Banta Singh.

'What? That's a lot of money. How did it happen?' demands his wife.

---

[43]Shankar's Axiom: If a train is on time, it must be twenty-four hours late. (From P Shankar, a childhood friend with a ready wit.)

'Well, all of us were sitting at Bachittar's place watching the match on tv, and I bet five hundred rupees that the wicket-keeper would take an easy catch. The ^&%$^ dropped it.'

The wife waits for Banta to explain more, but Banta keeps quiet.

'You said you lost thousand rupees ... What about the other 500?' she asks.

'Then they showed the action replay, and I bet again, hoping this time at least the *nikamma* (incompetent) would catch it ... It was such an easy catch too,' says Banta.

Commentary

Desire and hope will trump clear thinking every time. Furthermore, the division between the virtual and the real is getting thinner with each passing day. If a two-year-old cricket match were showing on the screen (say from a DVR), how could you tell that it wasn't live (assuming the players were still active)?

Justajoo for Just a Shoe

A sardar was madly in love. He declared his devotion daily to the lady who was the object of his ardor. 'What do you want? I'll do anything for you.'

'I'd been hoping to get a pair of crocodile boots ...' she said one day.

'Leave it to me,' said the sardar. 'I won't return without them.'

Then he disappeared for several months. His family and friends became worried, and tried to search for him. They hired many private investigators, contacted friends and relatives across the globe, and all came up blank.

Then, finally, some UN wildlife agency's investigating team looking into the sudden disappearance of crocodiles in the Serengeti struck gold, so to speak. They spotted the sardarji standing on the banks of a river.

He was examining a dead crocodile. '^&%$^, you are the eightieth crocodile, you are also barefoot!'

Commentary

The joke itself is quite lame (no pun intended), revolving entirely around the identical English usage for the crocodile's own boots and those made of crocodile skin.

But it does have a larger story, which it shares with some others in this collection: At what point does one re-examine one's beliefs in the light of evidence?

Two equally strong arguments can be made. The *New York Times* recently carried the story of Sir Isaac Newton being an alchemist prior to his career as a physicist and mathematician. It is well known that many talented individuals of the Middle Ages were people who had spent their entire lifetimes trying to turn lead into gold. We scoff at them now for their misguided persistence. On the other hand, there was Thomas Alva Edison, inventor of the electric bulb, who is reported to have exclaimed, after finding that one of his experiments for a filament had failed, 'I have discovered nine hundred things that will not make a filament.'

What if Edison had decided to abandon his efforts after the first hundred attempts?

You're a persistent genius if it works, and a loony wacko if it doesn't. As John F Kennedy said, 'Victory has a hundred fathers but defeat is an orphan.'

The Eating Contest

At a fair, Banta Singh sees a sign that says, 'If you can eat fifty pooris in fifteen minutes, we give you a lifetime of all-you-can-eat free lunch at our restaurant.'

He decides to take up the challenge. To keep score the proprietor has a sliding ruler with numbers marked on it. Every poori that Banta eats, the proprietor moves the slider up by one notch.

At ten pooris in two minutes, the proprietor is mildly surprised the sardarji has come so far. The previous maximum at this stage was seven. At fifteen pooris, the proprietor is beginning to get a little concerned. At twenty-five he is seriously alarmed. If Banta wins he will eat out his restaurant in a week.

At thirty-five he is desperate.

At forty-five pooris and thirteen minutes he knows he has to do something. Meanwhile Banta is busy asking for the pooris to be properly fried, crisp, for more subzi, pickle, and so on. He has paid no attention to the scoreboard.

At forty-seven the shopkeeper has a brainwave. At forty-eight, instead of raising the slider a notch, he lowers it to read forty-six.

It is downhill after that.

Banta has eaten his fifty-fifth poori when he is told the score is thirty-nine. He knows something is wrong.

'Oye, how thirty-nine, I must have eaten at least fifty,' he says.

The proprietor tries to belittle this notion with something to the effect that Banta is hardly known as the Srinivasa Ramanujan[44] of Punjab.

Banta protests. He may be no math genius but knows he has surely had more than thirty-nine. A big argument follows.

In the end Banta says to the proprietor and the audience, *'Oye theek hai, theek hai, theek hai. Chal bae ke dobaara shuru kariye. Hun khush* (OK, OK, OK. Let's just sit down and start all over. Happy now)?'

Commentary

Oh for the cool ability to project endless reserves of strength even with one's back against the wall!

Much of war, or negotiation, is psychological. With the German army barely fifteen miles from Moscow during World War II, Josef Stalin is reported to have been on the phone, calmly discussing with his allies how Germany should be divided after the war. He probably knew German intelligence was listening in.

According to biographer Paul Johnson, after making his famous WWII speech to the British people, 'We shall fight on the beaches, we shall fight on the landing grounds, we shall fight in the fields and in the streets, we shall fight in the hills. We shall never surrender,'

---

[44]A prodigy and a legend in the world of mathematics from India.

Winston Churchill added, out of the microphone's reach, 'we shall fight with pitchforks and broomsticks, it's about all we've bloody got.'

We can admire Banta Singh's endless appetite, or his limitless confidence.

Either way, he clearly had the stomach!

No Confessingh

Banta and Santa find two unexploded bombs. Good citizens both, they decide to carry the bombs to the nearest police station to hand them over for safe disposal. On the way Santa has a doubt.

'*Oye Banteya*, what if one of the bombs explodes?'

'*Oye tuon befiqar reh* (don't you worry). Simple. We'll just tell them we found one bomb.'

Commentary

We all play multiple roles in life, sometimes even several during the same day. Sometimes this switching of gears from one role to the next is rougher than expected. Here Banta and Santa were perhaps more accustomed to defend their actions to the authorities rather than playing public benefactor.

Napoleon the Careless

'Napoleon says, "My dictionary does not contain the word IM-POS-SI-BLE!,"' the inspirational speaker roared, pounding his fist on the podium while spitting out each syllable.

As the audience shook its head in dutiful awe, there arose from the back of the hall a voice. *'Oye hun roan da fayada kee?'* said the sardar, matter-of-factly, speaking more to himself than to others. 'Dictionary *khareedun toun pehle vekhna si* (what's the use of crying about it now? He should have checked before he bought the dictionary).'

Commentary

Close to the sardar's version of 'But the (French) emperor has nothing at all on.' Moral: Imagery is all well and good, but there is also such a notion as brass-tacks.

Benefits of Late Risingh

'OK, Banta, at 5 a.m. tomorrow morning you are going to be hanged,' says the jailer, bidding him goodnight one evening.

Banta laughs.

'What's so funny?' asks the jailer.

'Oye, I don't even get up before nine every morning!'

Commentary

I read somewhere that the word 'laconic' comes from the Spartan region of Laconia. When Philip of Macedon threatened the Spartans with, 'If I enter Laconia, I will raze Sparta to the ground,' their single-word reply was, 'If.'

Whether it was a foolhardy response or arose from a deep fearlessness it is impossible to say. In some ways it is entirely irrelevant. What counts is the complete equanimity in the face of imminent death.

As history recounts, the number of Sikh freedom fighters who went to the gallows in British India outnumbers that from any other community. Legendary figures such as Sardar Bhagat Singh actually mounted the hanging platform with a smile on their lips.

The Foreigner

Returning from a trip abroad Banta Singh asks his wife, '*Oye biwi, tainnu main firangi lagda waan* (hey, wife, do I look like a foreigner to you)?'

'*Bilkul nahin ji* (not at all),' she replies, pinching his cheeks playfully. '*Tussi ta* hundred percent Indian *ho.*'

'Hmmm ... *pata nahi valayat'ch saare* ^&%$^ *mainnu ae hoi puchch riye sun* (abroad everybody kept on asking me) – are you foreigner, are you foreigner, are you foreigner ...'

Commentary

Context is everything. The same sentence, the same word, the same expression, used in two different contexts, acquires a totally different complexion. Sometimes it is not a person who changes, but the circumstances. The results are the same. This is what causes remarks like, 'I feel like a foreigner in my own land.'

This is a story I heard from a friend of mine in California. During the heyday of the Y2K problem, when a number of Indian software engineers had been imported into the San Francisco Bay Area, it was not uncommon to find entire apartment complexes inhabited literally a hundred percent by Indian families. One day, an American worker knocked on one of the apartments asking for someone called 'John Matheson'. The lady of the house, who answered the door, told him that no such person lived in the apartment. When he thanked her and said he would try next door, she called out helpfully, 'In this whole complex, all Indians only, no foreigners!'

Déjà viewing

A sardar went to see the newly released Hollywood film, an MGM picture. As soon as the movie began, there was a picture of the MGM lion, turning its head and roaring.

He got up in disgust and strode out, saying, 'Bah, it's an old movie. I've already seen this one.'

Commentary

I've watched hundreds of people laugh at this joke, and wondered if there was some truth in the saying, we laugh loudest at those that resemble us the most.

Most of our lives are so profoundly repetitive that it is refreshing to see somebody who even recognizes the staidness of it all. People spend a substantial time of their lives watching soap operas or sitcoms, most of them indistinguishable, not to say undistinguished.

There is a good chance, had he sat through the opening instead of leaving the hall when he did, that the sardarji would have been treated to a plot very similar to one he had seen before – perhaps a love triangle, maybe a car chase, or even the special effects of several rounds of ammunition going off at once.

He probably figured that while he had already wasted his money, should he waste his time as well?

Torchbearer

After finishing his degree and getting his medical license, the sardarji set up practice. He was thrilled to see his first patient.

He welcomed him and sat him down with great courtesy. Then he took out his flashlight and carefully examined his ears, peering into them one by one while shining the torch inside.

Then he asked the patient to open his eyes wide, and holding the eyelids apart with one hand, shone the light into

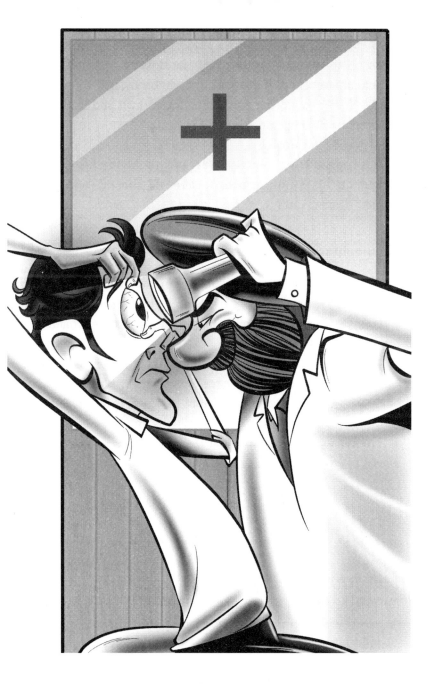

each eye, and nodded with a smile. After that he turned the torch on to look at the inside of the nose.

Finally he asked the patient to open his mouth wide, saying 'AAAAA'. He shone the torch into the mouth and nodded his head again, saying, 'Looks good.'

Then he sat down.

He opened his desk drawer and took out his pad. He picked up his fountain pen, unscrewed the lid, and slowly wrote, 'Torch is OK.'

Commentary

The patient and doctor are reading from two different scripts, as the saying goes; approaching the issue with different priorities, at any rate. Seemingly examining the patient, the doctor actually was testing his flashlight!

The Hindi expression for this sort of thing is *'apna ulloo seedha karna'*, used almost exactly as the corresponding English idiom, 'having one's axe to grind'. It is a microcosm of a pervasive problem in a society where responsibilities and positions are commonly viewed as a means to self-advancement at least as much as their avowed or official role or purpose.

The French Connection

An elderly sardarji was admitted to the ICU. During his long recovery after being often at death's door, he became very friendly with the attending doctor.

One day sardarji said to the doctor, 'Doctor sahib, after my recent experience, I want to learn French as quickly as possible.'

'Why, sardarji?' asked the doctor, a little surprised by this statement.

'French is the language of heaven, doctor sahib,' replied the sardar, 'and I want to be able to communicate with everyone there after I die.'

The doctor gave a smile, and thought he would play devil's advocate (no pun intended). 'But sardar sahib, they say there is also hell, after all. Just for the sake of argument, what if you happen to go there instead? How will you communicate in that case?' he asked.

'No problem then, doctor sahib,' came the answer. 'I speak fluent Punjabi.'

Commentary

Optimism in the face of adversity is the hallmark of a champion. Not only that he is going to heaven, assuredly the common belief of every believer, but the enthusiasm to learn an entirely alien language! What spirit!

How Time Flies

Banta Singh calls the airline. 'What is the flight time between Delhi and Amritsar?' he wants to know.

'Just one second ...' says the operator and goes to look up the information.

'OK, thank you,' says Banta Singh and puts the phone down.

Commentary

The joke here is that Banta Singh seems to have no concept of what might constitute a reasonable answer to his question.

He need not feel too bad – he is hardly alone; indeed one might say he is in exalted company. When US President George W Bush wanted to invade Iraq, he and his advisers estimated the overall cost to be US $60 billion,[45] and that the whole affair would be concluded in a matter of months. In reality, five years later the war was still on, had cost US $600 billion by official reckoning, and even pegged as high as US $4 trillion taking into account long-term costs, according to a Nobel Prize-winning economist!

Pie ji

Banta Singh was ordering a large pizza over the phone. After taking down all the instructions about toppings – onion, tomato, chicken and more, the pizza clerk asked, 'How many slices, sir, should I cut it into six or twelve pieces?'

---

[45]'Estimates of Iraq War Cost Were Not Close to Ballpark' by David M Herszenhorn, *New York Times*, 19 March 2008. This is aside from the moral turpitude involved in launching the war.

'Oh, six, please. Just six. I could never eat twelve pieces.'

Commentary

A profound joke.

It illustrates the truth that we commit (and accept) a number of things by changing their names – the more 'modern' we get, we seem to increasingly fall for our own ruses. For example, it might be hard to tell a man he no longer has a job, but saying 'the company is downsizing' makes it a lot easier, even to the person losing his job. A weapon to kill thousands is thus called a 'Peacemaker' or 'Daisy Cutter'.

I had a college friend who thought, genuinely, that referring to his servant as his 'helper' somehow changed the relationship.

Those in advertising and public relations have known this for decades.

Banta Singh's Alphabet

A for Apple
B for Bante da Apple
C for Chota Apple
D for Dooja Apple
E for Ik hore Apple
F for Faddo Apple
G for Gol Apple
H for Hara Apple

I for Idda Apple
J for Jidda Apple
K for Kidda Apple
L for Lae vai Apple
M for Mota Apple
N for Navan Apple
O for Orange
P for Pra da Apple
Q for Qual'ty Apple
R for Rad (red) Apple
S for Sante da Apple
T for Twadda Apple
U for Udda Apple
V for V'layati Apple
W for Wadda Apple
X for Axtra (extra) Apple
Y for Yellow (yellow) Apple
Z for Z'meen par Apple

Santa Singh's Alphabet

A for Aelephaint
B for B'fallow
C for K'bootar
D for Dunkey
E for Eppal

F for F'looda
G for Ji-huzoor
H for H'ramzade
I for Aish
J for Jugaad
K for K'maal
L for Lainch
M for Min't
N for Nede
O for O'ye
P for Puttar
Q for Kyoon?
R for Rapta
S for S'cand
T for Thalle
U for Utte
V for V'layat
W for Do Ulloo
X for Kullad
Z for Zad

Name Change?

Many years ago when Banta Singh was being admitted to primary school, an unfortunate incident took place that would plague him the rest of his life.

The clerk had his head down, entering all his details into the admissions register. He had just written 'Banta Singh' for the first and middle names of the child. 'Last name,' he called out. Just then, Banta's dad, who was supplying all the information, happened to notice that little Banta had flung his shoes away somewhere. '*Nange* (bare)?' he scolded Banta, pointing to his feet.

The clerk, his head still buried in the fat register, caught some of this exchange and absentmindedly wrote down, '*Nange*' as the last name. And there it was, cast in stone – for life.

Nange, as you may know, also means 'nude' in Punjabi.

Life became difficult for poor Banta from then on. The school record followed him wherever he went, and at every future institution he dealt with: school, college, job, even at rail and plane counters, everyone laughed at his name, which was, after all, officially Banta Singh Nange.

'*Oye Banteya*, why don't you just change your official name and solve this problem once and for all,' a good-natured colleague finally suggested to him one day.

Banta thought this was a wonderful idea. He wondered why he hadn't thought of it himself. The very next day he petitioned the court with a Change of Name application.

Like everyone else who heard or saw his name for the first time, the judge also took one look at it and burst out laughing. 'Banta Singh Nange! Ho ho ho. Ha ha.'

After a couple of minutes, restraining his mirth and a little embarrassed at having lost his composure on the bench in this fashion, the judge said, in a serious tone, 'OK, Sardar Banta Singh Nange, *assan kee kariye twadde vaste* (what can we do for you)?'

'Your honor, all my life people have laughed at my name. I am tired of it. I want to change it,' Banta Singh said with feeling.

'I don't blame you at all, *puttar*,'[46] said the judge, now genuinely contrite and sympathetic. 'I am here to help you. We will do it right away. Have you picked your new name?'

'Yes, your honor,' said Banta Singh, smiling for the first time in the proceedings.

'Well, what is your wish?' asked the judge, expansively.

'Santa Singh Nange.'

Commentary

People can go through their entire lives blaming one incident, or job, or person, or some specific circumstance, for their ill-fate and misfortune. Often a person's own view of his situation and its causes can be skewed, and quite at variance with how others see it. Even the blame of a lifetime can sometimes be entirely misplaced.

We've Got it Covered

Banta Singh was on his first trip abroad visiting his friend in New York, and the friend was showing him around Central Park. Suddenly they saw people running away from somewhere, quite in a panic. His friend asked one of the frightened runners what was going on.

---

[46]Son.

'Man, there's a mugger out there,' the fellow replied. 'He has an AIDS-infected syringe and says he'll poke you with it if you don't give up your wallet,' he added, before hurrying away.

Banta thought for a moment, told his friend to stay where he was, and that he would be right back. Then he left, walking down the street briskly.

He returned in a few minutes. People were still running away from the mugger. Ignoring his friend's pleas and those of others around, Banta Singh headed straight to where they said the man was.

His friend and others followed him at a distance, trying to ask him to come back but also curious as to what he would do.

Then they saw the mugger, brandishing the needle. But the mugger clearly did not expect anyone to be so bold as to approach him. Banta Singh just went right up to him, gave him a slap that sent the needle flying, then pinned his arms behind his back and hauled him out. Along the way he also gave him a short lesson in Punjabi *gaalis*.

The entire crowd at Central Park, and the police sharpshooters who had been ready to fire, applauded the act and cheered. The mugger was taken into custody.

Thereafter Banta Singh was the darling of all the news channels. This visitor from India, who was so brave and unassuming, was the hero of the hour.

'When all the others were panicking, how did you dare go near this guy? He could have infected you with AIDS,' one newscaster asked.

'No problem, madam. There was never any danger to me,' said our hero, with assurance.

'How can you say that?' she asked, her eyes glowing in admiration.

'*Mai poori time caandem paya hoya si* (I was wearing a condom throughout),' he replied.

Commentary

Faith (or belief, a less fraught word), is an amazing thing, independent of whether its object is true or not. There are many examples, both in real life and in fiction, of people doing things under its influence they would not normally consider themselves capable of doing – things good and bad.

Bullet Proof

Tension was mounting. During the last Indo-Pak war, an Indian army unit was holed up behind a rise. They had come upon an enemy unit, which was also lying in wait for them. Both sides were on the alert.

Suddenly, Banta Singh was seen running up and down between the two frontlines, waving his arms in the air and shouting. He was unarmed but wearing a mosquito net over his combat fatigues.

The other side was completely puzzled. They couldn't help getting up to see what had happened. When they were thus distracted, the Indian unit rushed towards them and captured their position without major injuries on either side.

Banta Singh was hailed as a hero by his entire company.

'You were stupid, though I'm happy it all turned out okay. You could have been riddled with bullets,' said his CO.

'Sirjee, *mai sochaya jadon aeddi chotti machchar ae de vichon lang nahin sakdi ta goli kisnaan ghusoo* (sir, I reasoned, when a tiny mosquito cannot penetrate this net, how could a large bullet)?'

'OK, OK,' said the CO, relieved that things had not gone as badly wrong as they could have. 'But don't you ever try this again.'

The logic was not lost on his comrade and buddy Santa Singh, also serving in the same unit, who happened to overhear this conversation.

A few days later there was a similar confrontation. The air was taut with anticipation. Firing could break out any moment. Each side was waiting for the other to make a move.

A nude figure suddenly started dancing in the space between the frontlines. This was Santa Singh.

This was irresistible to the other side (another company; the previous one had been captured, remember?) and taking advantage of their distraction, Santa and Banta's company scored another victory.

'You lucky fool. You could have been riddled with bullets,' the CO thundered.

'No, sirjee. *Mai ta* Odomos *paya hoya si* (I was wearing Odomos),'[47] came the answer.

---

[47]Odomos is a popular Indian brand of mosquito repellant cream.

Commentary

Faith again. Twice in a row.

As to the argument that a bullet could scarcely get through where a little mosquito could not, I listened in slack-jawed disbelief recently to an almost identical line of reasoning being advanced in all seriousness by Gen Pervez Musharraf, former president of Pakistan. Asked in a television interview[48] whether it was conceivable that Osama bin Laden could have remained hidden in a fortified city like Abbottabad without the knowledge of the Pakistani establishment, Musharraf provided the following 'proof'. Ask around Bin Laden's compound, he said. The children in the area, all of whom would have recognized Bin Laden in a photograph, did not know that he was staying there. In that case, the general asked in the manner of one who has clinched his case, how can you expect the Pakistani security to know he was there!

Museum Piece

A young student and his father are among the dozens of visitors admiring the magnificently preserved bones of a stegosaurus at the Natural History Museum.

'How old is that skeleton, Papa?' asks the boy.

---

[48]Watch this segment (around 1:05 minutes into the interview) at http://www.youtube.com/watch?v=LPnD3bhW8BM.

The father doesn't know. 'Very old. Very, very old, son,' he says, tentatively.

Banta Singh, who is the guard at the exhibit, is listening to the conversation. 'Actually, sirjee, it is one-hundred-and twenty-five million and sixteen years, thirty-three days old,' he says.

All the visitors to the exhibit are struck dumb by such precise knowledge – that too from a mere guard.

Finally someone asks him, 'But, sir, how are you so sure of the exact number, right to the day?'

'*Oye it is simpal* (hey it's simple),' answers Banta Singh. 'You see, I asked the same question the day I joined, and the museum curator told me the skeleton was one-hundred-and-twenty-five million years old. Now, I have been with this museum for exactly sixteen years and thirty-three days ...'

Commentary

We may laugh, but can we say that Banta Singh was wrong?

After all, mixing individual perspective, myth, history, and reality has been the stock-in-trade of the post-modern discourse for some decades. And now Banta Singh stands vindicated by no less an institution than the Allahabad High Court, one of whose judges ruled recently on the exact spot where Lord Rama[49] had been born!

---

[49] A Hindu god, an avatar in Indian mythology.

Getting Ahead

The sardar came to the doctor with a big bump on his forehead.

'What happened?' asked the doctor, as he tended to the wound.

'Doctor sahib, I was just doing my work,' he answered.

'What kind of work do you do, sardarji?' the doctor asked.

'Sirjee, I break rocks with a hammer.'

'Oh, I see. And a rock fell on your head, or the hammer accidentally hit your head …' the doctor surmised.

'No, No, doctor sahib. It was my supervisor who told me to do it.'

'What?'

'Yes, doctor sahib. He was walking by inspecting everybody's work. After watching me breaking stones with the hammer he said, "Oye sardar, use your head at least once in a while." '

Commentary

Taking things literally usually has its pitfalls, but rarely entails physical harm as in this case. Still, while we may fault the sardar for missing the message here, clearly his boss is no communication wizard either. An essential component of management is knowing with whom to use metaphors and when to stick to plain and simple words.

Towering Over Bachittar

Banta and Bachittar are on their first visit to the big city, each looking every bit the curious bumpkin. As they are walking along the causeway their attention is suddenly arrested by the sight of tall buildings the likes of which they've never seen before.

As they stand there counting the number of floors in each skyscraper, a couple of truant college students, who have been watching them from a distance, approach them deciding to have some fun.

'First visit to the city, correct?' one of them asks, assuming the breezy air of a man in-charge.

'*Aho ji* (yes, sir),' comes the cautious answer.

'That's what I thought. Do you know there's a charge to look at those buildings?'

'Sirjee, *sannu nahi pata si* (we didn't know that, sir),' replies Banta.

'Now you know. Which *manzil* (floor) were you looking at?' the man asks, turning to Bachittar.

'Twenty-fourth,' replies Bachittar.

'OK, note down, twenty-fourth floor, twenty rupees per floor, that makes it four-hundred-and-eighty rupees. Give him a receipt,' he says to his sidekick, as Bachittar counts out four-hundred and four twenty rupee bills and forks them over.

'OK, sardarji, what about you?' the prankster says, turning to Banta, emboldened by his unexpected success.

'Fifth floor,' said Banta.

'Really, just fifth? Hard to believe. But OK, we'll take you at your word. Give him a receipt for hundred rupees,' he snaps to his associate, who is scribbling hastily on his college notebook and tearing out the sheet to hand to the villagers.

Happy with their unexpected bounty the college students leave.

Banta turns to Bachittar. '*Oye tuon jithe vi aan rahna* ^&%$^ *ohoi pindaan da* (wherever you may go you'll ^&%$^ remain a villager). *Kee lode si chouvee manzil kahandee khamokhan* (where was the need to say twenty-fourth floor needlessly)? *Tainnu pata e? Main vekh riya si tee manzil nu. Par mai ki dassaya onnanu? Panj* (did you know? I was staring at the thirtieth floor. But what did I tell them? Fifth)! *Hun tuon vi z'ra chant ban ja* (now you too need to smarten up a little).'

Commentary

Some questions cannot be answered, they can only be themselves questioned, rejected or ignored *in toto* – a prime example of such verbal traps being the classic, 'When did you stop beating your wife?' Those falling into the trap don't realize there is no 'right answer' that will free them – the very act of answering of such questions is one's undoing.

The larger point is that sometimes it is ridiculous to get into the details; they must be avoided completely.

As an ancient Jewish saying has it, the difference between the wise man and the clever man is that the clever man can extricate himself from a situation into which the wise man never would have gotten himself in the first place.

Not cleverness but wisdom is the way out.

Another point. Banta and Bachittar are equally new to the city. Yet Banta speaks with such authority to Bachittar about the ways of the metropolis, pulling rank based on his seniority in the village, not realizing he is as much a dupe as the other in this instance. I've always been struck by a similar equation, particularly in the days before cable tv and the internet, between Indian parents visiting their sons in the US. The husband would continue his role as the 'enlightened one', lecturing (and hectoring) the wife on matters with which both were equally unfamiliar.

Sometimes the luxury of saying, 'I don't know' is so casually discarded that one can only pity the person who does so.

X-Ray-ted

On his way back from work one day Banta Singh sees a crowd assembled on the sidewalk near his bus stop. At the center of the hubbub is an itinerant salesman. He is hawking something fancy, it appears. Curious to know what he is selling, Banta wiggles his way close to the front.

It turns out that the salesman is selling X-Ray spectacles. They look exactly like normal glasses, he says, but with them on you can see through anybody's clothes. They are the same kind the security people at American airports are using these days, but at a bargain price.

But what does it do to the eyes, Banta finds himself wondering. As if in answer to his question, the salesman says, 'If you find it disorienting, just take off the spectacles, and everything starts appearing normal again. As simple as that.'

After a lot of bargaining, Banta Singh buys a pair of X-Ray spectacles. At least it will provide some fun at home, he reasons.

Eager to show them to his wife, he enters his house silently, deciding to surprise her. He tiptoes upstairs and puts them on just before entering the bedroom.

What should he see but his wife and his best friend in what the Indian newspapers in the old days used to call, 'a compromising position'.

They are not wearing any clothes. Banta Singh notices this too ... and is quite gratified. The X-Ray spectacles were definitely worth the money!

He takes off the glasses. But he finds his wife and his friend, both too startled by this intrusion to cover themselves, still in their birthday suits.

Banta turns livid – at the guy who sold him the spectacles.

'Ae ta ^&%$^ bandal cheez e (this is a bloody useless thing) ^&%$^, I took off the glasses, but my eyes are still stuck on nanga (nude) mode. ^&%$^ X-Ray wale ne mainnu Chinese maal fada'tta (the ^&%$^ X-Ray guy cheated me, I think he stuck me with a Chinese[50] model)!'

Commentary

Preoccupation is preemption of thought, as we can see from this bizarre story. Banta Singh is so caught up in his new toy that he does not

---

[50]Chinese goods are considered of inferior quality in India.

even notice his wife's infidelity. Instead, he is focused on the vendor's assurance that his vision will return to normal once he takes off the glasses. Basically, he is inside a completely different narrative.

In a deeper sense, presented with many different explanations for a particular phenomenon, we often choose the one that least requires us to change our mindset. Rather than face the bitter reality in front of his eyes, Banta Singh goes for the ready scapegoat, 'Chinese made'.

Railway Crossingh

'What time does the GT arrive today?' Banta Singh asks the man at the inquiry counter at the railway station.

'7:15,' he replies.

'And Rajdhani?'

'7:35.'

'What about Sh'tabdi?'

'7:45. Anything else?' asks the clerk, a little irritated.

'*Sirf ik hore, ji* (just one more, sir) ... Punjab Mail *kinne baje* (what time)?'

'Please don't waste my time. Can't you see so many people waiting in line behind you? Sardarji, for heaven's sake ... where do you actually want to go?'

'Oh, I live right here across the railway line and was walking home. I just wanted to cross the tracks safely,' says Banta Singh.

Commentary

It is common experience that many things are used for purposes completely different from their original design. For example, it is a tribute to talk of a habitually punctual individual by saying one could set one's watch by his arrival. The person himself may not be aware of this dependence. In cultures where large institutions are the only ones that go by any predictable routine, it is customary to rely on them to regulate a variety of other schedules, quite unbeknownst to them. This saves numerous individuals and smaller institutions the trouble of investing in their own time systems.

Many decades ago in India, there was a betting scheme based on what to its organizers was an entirely random outcome, namely the last digit of the closing price of cotton in the New York Exchange. Few people in India would have any interest in this statistic for any commercial reason. But the Indian newspapers would make it a point to print this, because there was a large betting public which demanded it!

So long as it is not malicious or illegal, it is an excellent idea to piggyback on the service of an existing institution. However, in many societies this is carried out on such a scale that it affects the service itself. Regard for appropriate use of the 'commons' is a sign of a developed society.

Plus ça Bus da change

A bus fell into a raging river. A few passengers were somehow rescued, among them Banta Singh. After searching frantically along the shore for a few minutes, he jumped back into the river, to the horror of all the other passengers.

Somehow they rescued him a second time. 'What happened? Family members?' the rescuer asked.

'*Na ji*. Conductor %^%$ change *vapas nahin ditta si* (the bloody conductor hadn't returned my change) ...'

Commentary

> 'Once in a while you will stumble upon the truth but most
> of us manage to pick ourselves up and hurry along as if
> nothing had happened.'
>
> –Winston Churchill

The mind is an inherently petty piece of work. Even an encounter with death, which one might presume would perforce instill a perspective on what is important in life, rarely deters it from its métier – the active pursuit of the trivial.

Sound on Logic, Light on Theory

Teacher: Class, can anyone tell me, why do we see the lightning before we hear the thunder?

Banta Singh: Because our eyes are in front and ears are at the back.

Commentary

The joke is a 'thundering' indictment of book knowledge.

Banta's is as good a commonsense explanation as any, and hardly dissimilar to many other explanations for various phenomena which we accept unquestioningly when handed down in print. It also illustrates the rather ridiculous fealty people express for some recently heard scientific 'truth', which they themselves can neither prove nor disprove (or often, even understand) and which is likely to be debunked by some other paper just a few years down the road. The stuff is irrelevant to most people's lives.

'What the deuce is it to me ... you say that we go round the sun. If we went round the moon it would not make a pennyworth of difference to me or to my work,' says Sherlock Holmes to Watson, when the latter is surprised to find him 'ignorant of the Copernican Theory and the composition of the solar system'.

As Swami Vivekananda said admiringly of the lowest of Indians, '... Ask a man, "Who are the English?" — he does not know ... "Who governs you?" We do not know. "What is the government?" They do not know. But they know philosophy.'

A faculty that a post-modern education system, seduced by gadgetry and reduced to the notion that the internet contains the answer to every question if only you work a search engine hard enough, seems to have leached away.

Auto-convinsingh

Banta Singh wanted to sell his car when it reached 100,000 miles. He had heard the resale value drops rapidly thereafter. He sought out a knowledgeable friend in the car business to seek his advice. The friend seconded the idea but, being not too particular about ethics, suggested a scheme: Banta could roll back the odometer to 50,000 miles, so he could get a better offer. In fact, he knew a back-alley mechanic who would do this for eighty rupees. Banta was at first hesitant, but he agreed finally; and the deed was done.

Some weeks later the friend ran into Banta Singh again, and inquired if the car had been sold.

'Sold?' asked Banta, incredulous. 'Yaar, *kaa di chchetti payi e* (what's the hurry)? It only has got 50,000 miles!'

Commentary

'Don't drink your own kool-aid,' goes the American warning. Which is to say, don't fall for your own propaganda. As the notorious Indian outlaw Charles Sobhraj admonished his brother, you can tell others all the lies you want, just don't ever start believing them yourself.

But here Banta Singh has a point too. Depreciation is a universal accounting technique to properly value what someone would pay for a piece of equipment, so as to gather a realistic estimate of an organization's assets. If in its current state a prospective buyer would fall for the 50,000-mile ruse, is that not validation enough?

Such self-deception happens often in the software world. The user interface is snazzy, so the company thinks the product is great, forgetting the rot underneath. Announcement and release follow. Reality – and version 2.0 – catches up later!

The Oldest Sardar Joke – Revised and Extended

A sardar is sunbathing on a pleasant day in Goa. There are plenty of American tourists at the beach that day, and from time to time, a passing tourist smiles and tries to make conversation, beginning with, 'Are you relaxing?'

To which the sardar dutifully replies, stifling each time his increasing irritation, 'No, I am Milkha Singh.'

[This is probably the first sardar joke I ever heard. Who says jokes cannot be improved? I came by an updated version recently ... read on ...]

After being disturbed a few times in this manner, the sardar decides to shift to another spot. As he moves across to a different section of the beach some distance away he crosses another sardar stretched out under an umbrella.

'*Sab changa ji* (all going well)?' he greets the reclining sardar as he walks past.

'*Aho ji, bilkul* (yes, sir, absolutely),' replies the other sardar, smiling. '*Aethe 'raam hi 'raam e* (it's totally comfortable here). I am relaxing.'

The first sardar stops dead in his tracks. Suddenly he is angry.

'*Oye yaar Relak Singh, loki saare othe tainnu th'oohnd rahe haan, tuon* ^&%$^ *aithe 'raam kee kar riya e* (hey man Relak Singh, everybody is looking for you over there; what the ^&%$^ are you doing stretched out here)?'

Commentary

A perfect finale. Who would gild a lily?

Acknowledgments

Khushwant Singh provided kind counsel at the outset.

Roopinder Singh and Aakar Patel made me believe *Bantaism* might one day actually be published.

Jeji Anna, Mala Manni, Sridhar, Chinu, Anand Rajaram, Vijay Char and Meenakshi Sanyal – all waved me on; Sridhar troubling to provide page-wise critiques, Vijay capturing the spirit of the effort perfectly with his phrase, 'an ode not a slur'.

Sucharita and her Punjabi-enthusiast husband Ananthanarayanan thought to get me in touch with Bakhtiar Dadabhoy. Poor Bakhtiar trudged through the entire manuscript before recommending it to the folks at Rupa.

Editor Shikha is a model of quiet efficiency and competence, a pleasure to work with. Artist Nitin Chawla seems to read my mind from halfway across the globe.

With their support, love and care my wife and children have made a difficult time seem almost normal. C'mon, you know what I mean …

In lives of simplicity and sacrifice Amma and Perima remain constants in a topsy-turvy world, just as Appa's memory continues to awe, inspire, and chasten.

Long, long ago, fellow workers at the 'Ikkohi' Bank in Delhi put me through an unwitting Punjabi *visarjan* (immersion), as it slowly began to register that here was no mere language but an entire take on Existence, a construction immortalized by KS *'Damaag jutte'ch te hath'ch talwar'* Dinesh.

Earlier still on an idle college afternoon, Ashok Sharma, *Le Duc de Green Park,* first introduced me to Banta Singh. *Balihari guru aap no,* etc.